MW01592855

HOW DO YOU KNOW?

A Guide to Clear Thinking About Wall Street, Investing, & Life

Christopher Mayer

Foreword by Bill Bonner

 BONNER & PARTNERS

Printed in the United States of America
First Edition

ISBN 978-0-692-99683-6

Bonner & Partners
55 NE 5th Avenue, Suite 100
Delray Beach, Florida 33483

Cover by:
Matthew Mayer

www.bonnerandpartners.com

Table of Contents

PART I

Ways of Knowing

PART II

Devices for Clear Thinking

PART III

Chapel Perilous

Foreword

Nobody Knows Anything

By Bill Bonner

Chris Mayer is a great partner. While I focus on the nature of money, theoretical economics, the rigged macro system, and increasingly politics, Chris turns his attention to a very practical matter: investing. That is, he has the responsibility for real money of real people in the real world.

How should you approach your investments? How should you think about them?

I have only general and theoretical answers: Keep a substantial amount in cash and gold... stay out of bonds... avoid the U.S. "stock market." And when everyone thinks he has figured out a way to get rich, bet against them all!

As you will see in the pages that follow, these general instructions – as good as they might be – take on new meaning when you begin to look more closely at the details.

Through a series of provocative – and often amusing – examples, Chris puts those perennial investing questions into a much larger context... How do you know anything at all? His answer, which is sure to make many readers uncomfortable... You don't.

Chris writes: "For every assertion, there are qualifications; for every belief, there are reasons to doubt; and for every theory, there is potential for revision, if not eventual rejection entirely."

For example, it is all very well to recognize that the financial system has been corrupted by phony money and mispriced credit. This insight might well lead you, as it did me, to want to keep your distance. "The prices quoted for stocks and bonds do not reflect the real value of the businesses that stand behind them," we might say to one another. We might conclude that only fools would buy assets in such a tricked-up market.

That conclusion – right as it may be – can be a very expensive one. Since 2009, the S&P 500 is up about 200%. The Dow has jumped from around 7,000 to over 22,000. And those of us who refused to go along "lost" a lot of money.

I put "lost" in quotation marks because a missed opportunity is not the same as money down the drain. It's one thing to have it and lose it. It's quite another to never get it. And when you do get it – either from investing, business, career, or inheritance – the last thing you want to do is lose it.

Still, the point is: The investing world is full of theories... But you shouldn't invest theoretically. You can do a lot of thinking about it in an abstract or theoretical way. Some of this thinking can help you understand what may be going on. But much of it can mislead you, as Chris will show you.

Either way, it's not broad theory that brings you money; it's something very specific. A specific insight. A specific business. Or a specific investment. Every situation is different. As Chris reminds us, turning an old maxim on its head:

> This time is *always* different. And every time is always different from every other time. Episodes may seem similar on the surface or in certain important ways, but there are countless details that are different from prior episodes. And you cannot be sure those details don't matter.

And every idea has to be suitable to a specific investor at a specific time.

The investor who needs his money in five years for his retirement is very different from the investor who plans to pass on his portfolio, untouched, to his grandchildren. If the broad market of stocks is in a downswing, the person who needs the money in five years might be simply out of luck. He should not 'fight the tape,' as the old timers say.

On the other hand, the person with the long investment horizon might continue on his way, regardless of the tape. Typically, the long-term investor looks for value and doesn't care much about when he finds it. He can wait for it to reveal itself.

"Volatility" is also a serious threat to the short-term investor. His investments may be down when he needs to sell them. But volatility can be a benefit for the long-term investor. He can wait for a downswing, buy, and then hold on until he is ready to sell into a rising market.

How Do You Know?

It is a matter of perspective, as Chris emphasizes repeatedly in these pages.

But *How Do You Know?* is not another book on investing. It is full of ideas about investing, including one that hasn't been part of the public investing discussion in nearly 60 years. But Chris' goal is not just to give you ideas, but to provide practical guidelines for uncluttering your thinking – that is, for getting unhelpful ideas and misleading information out of the way.

You cannot learn enough in the popular press to make sense of what's going on in the world... let alone make a sensible investment. Besides, the media, the financial industry, and regulators – all have their own motivations and favored narratives. None really wants to help you get rich.

One makes money by selling you investments. Obviously, if he thought the investment would be a huge success, he'd keep it for himself. Another makes money by selling advertising to the companies who are selling you investments. Rarely will journalists uncover the small company without an ad budget that is going to go up 100 times.

You need to be a little suspicious of what you see on TV, read in the media, or get from the financial industry. It is often distorted by their own self-interest... that is, by the desire to sell you something. I'm not talking here about conflicts of interest. There is no conflict; neither the financial industry nor the media have any interest in making you money. The role of the media – to a serious investor – is to help him understand what other investors think, not what he should think.

Even if he has won the battle against groupthink, alas, the war is not over. Your most dangerous enemy is still on the field, fully armed, and full of tricks. That enemy is you. Psychologically, it is almost impossible to resist the public narratives. There are also our own prejudices, delusions, and desires.

"We see what we want to see" is the popular expression. If we are long stocks, we see a rising stock market. If we are short, we see calamity around the corner. And then, when we seem to be wrong, we tend to double down, as if to prove something. The result is usually to turn a small loss into a big one.

How do you win the battle against yourself? First, be aware that you are a very formidable opponent. Second, understand investment markets... statistical tricks...

and, as the ancient Greeks advised, 'know thyself' and the mischief your own emotions can get up to.

Most important: Work hard. A fundamental law of the universe tells us that the harder and longer you work at something, the more likely you are to get better-than-average results. So, it is not surprising, to me anyway, that Chris has consistently beaten the market, and done so by margins that would make Warren Buffett envious.

Hard work pays off. Research and study help you keep your wild, impulsive self in check and direct your investments to the specific assets that are most likely to go up. Careful study also gives you a healthy respect for uncertainty and appreciation for the risk it entails, as you'll see in what follows.

You will see, too, that almost the entire world seems to be living in a fantasy land. In markets and life, most people believe what isn't true: Stocks and real estate always go up in the long run... you can't change history... stocks have an "intrinsic value"... 1 plus 1 always equals 2... These are just a few of the many "myths" Chris picks apart as he shows how many of the 'facts' we thought we knew are not 'facts' at all.

"Nobody knows anything" is another old-timers' expression. Chris reminds us why this is so... and what to do about it – not just in investing... but in life.

Bill Bonner
Poitou, France
September 2017

Preface

"So, what is knowing, and what is knowledge? What do we mean when we say we know? ... Please, sirs, do go into this with me, pay a little attention. To *know* is a very interesting word. How do you know, and what do you know? Please ask yourselves, as I am asking myself."

~ Jiddu Krishnamurti (1895-1986), philosopher

How do you know?

In this book, we'll ask this question often and in different ways. We'll look at how we can think about it and use it to take apart all kinds of problems, financial and otherwise. The goal is to help clarify your thinking.

As for an answer to the question itself, I don't think I'm giving too much away if I give it to you now: You don't know – not for sure. And you can't know – not nearly as much as you think you can. But to have an idea about these boundaries is the beginning of wisdom...

Introduction
Abracadabra: You Create With Words

"The real secret of magic is that the world is made of words, and that if you know the words that the world is made of you can make of it whatever you wish."

~ Terence McKenna (1946-2000), lecturer and author of *True Hallucinations*

"I think that the most pervasive and fundamental of these obstacles to change and growth is a complicated condition we can call by a simple name... 'a belief in magic.' I think we *all* believe in magic."

~ Wendell Johnson (1906-1965), psychologist and author of *People in Quandaries*

Abracadabra.

The word, Aramaic in origin, means, "I create with words." (This is one theory among several for the origin and meaning of the phrase. As with so many things, it is a matter of contention.) Its associations with magic are all too apt.

As you'll see, investing (and life) is full of tricks and illusions based on little more than word magic. This book, in a sense, is a guide to breaking these spells.

For much of what we think about Wall Street, investing, and life rests on nothing more than abstractions – words and symbols (and words are a kind of symbol) – that have no basis in the world "out there." In short, we make them up. They exist in our heads only. And yet we come to treat them as if they were real.

In doing so, we deceive ourselves and allow others to deceive us. We waste a lot of time on pointless guesswork. We make avoidable thinking errors. We put our trust in bad maps and wander astray. In the markets, we lose money – and a piece of our sanity.

What we need is a radically different way to think about the world around us. We need a way of thinking mindfully of this abstracting and the limits of those abstractions.

Fortunately, such a way exists, though it seems largely forgotten except by a small group of connoisseurs. In what follows, I'll share with you this robust framework for identifying and piercing through these abstractions. I'll give you tools to sharpen your thinking. If you work with these tools, I guarantee you will see results. I can't guarantee you won't ever fall for magical thinking again. But you will fall for less magical nonsense than before.

Francis P. Chisholm (1905-1965), who taught at the State Teachers College in River Falls, Wisconsin, and who was an advocate of what I'm going to tell you about, spoke eloquently about its benefits in his *Introductory Lectures on General Semantics*.

Among the benefits:

- "Understanding and overcoming primitive and infantile linguistic habits such as word magic."

- Overcoming faulty thinking habits that underlie dogmatism, prejudice, etc.

- Removing "thought blockages" and bad reading habits.

- Awareness of silent assumptions, meanings, and beliefs.

As someone who has adopted this approach, I'd add at least a few more benefits:

- Deeper appreciation for the complexity of our world, the tenuous nature of cause and effect, and the limits of our knowledge.

- Skepticism regarding labels, names, and classifications.

- Greater sensitivity to differences.

- Awareness of the difficulty of escaping our own conceptual grids or "reality tunnels" (to use Timothy Leary's phrase).

To get us there, I've got a basketful of mental devices that will help protect you against spells and word magic. I'll share all of this with you in the pages that follow.

The thesis I advance here has a rich history and is radical in what it suggests, though initially it may seem obvious. When pursued to its logical ends, I assure you, the deeper implications are startling. And we will push them to their limits in what follows.

Magical words and symbols – Wall Street's spells – manifest themselves in various ways. I will highlight and categorize as many as I can think of.

I'll also add that the field here is open. The last book – and, so far as I know, the only book – to cover what I'm about to share with you came out in 1958. The original title was *The General Semantics of Wall Street* by John Magee. The book in your hands is the first effort to bring "general semantics" back to Wall Street and the investing public in 60 years. We'll get to what general semantics is all about in Chapter 1.

(As an aside, "Wall Street" itself is an abstraction. It exists as a place, but it is also a symbol – of greed, money, power, and more – as Mr. Magee pointed out in the first chapter of his book in 1958. We can't help but abstract, as I will point out more than once, but we can know when we're doing it and cultivate an awareness of abstracting and the limitations it entails.)

A Warm-Up: Some Examples to Show You Where We're Headed

I'll start with a few examples of abstractions, to give you a sense for where we're going. There are easy examples and then there are harder mind-bending examples. Let's start with a couple of easy ones.

In early 2017, Bloomberg carried a story titled "Value Investing Hits Back." The subtitle was "Growth stocks were favored, but it's not over yet."

The story kicks off this way:

> Value investing was supposed to be on the mat, waiting out its last few moments before it surrendered for good to growth stocks. But a curious thing happened in 2016; it got back up and rallied, and it looks as if it is prepared to continue the fight.

The proof offered for this thesis was the performance of various indexes, some labeled "value" and others labeled "growth." The "growth" indexes were ahead.

Here are a few of those bullets:

- MSCI USA Value Index beat MSCI USA Growth Index by 10.4 percent last year, including dividends.

- MSCI USA Small Cap Value Index beat MSCI USA Small Cap Growth Index by 11.8 percent.

- MSCI Emerging Markets Value Index beat MSCI Emerging Markets Growth Index by 7.6 percent.

Just reading this again I find the whole thing comical. I do not mean to pick on this particular writer or Bloomberg. Stories like this are as common as weeds. Nonetheless, I would submit to you this story has no value whatsoever.

What is the typical investor supposed to think after reading this? That there are two teams out there, "value" and "growth," like the New York Giants and Washington Redskins, vying for the top spot in some mystical financial division? What is "value investing"? What is "growth investing"? We are led to believe they are some readily identifiable things, as if you could go to the grocery store and pick them off the shelves.

The whole piece lends an air of certainty and definiteness to concepts that are foggy at best. "Value investing," for example, is a term that really has little meaning. It can include investors so different from each other that you have to question the validity of the term altogether. And the idea that there are "value stocks" and "growth stocks" is one of those tired old fictions I wish would go away. There is no such thing as a "value stock" or a "growth stock."

One man's growth stock is another man's value stock – and vice versa. In other words, people create these categories. And they create them using varying criteria, which they select. One stock can, therefore, fill many roles depending on the definition used; sometimes the same stock fulfills the same roles at the same time.

As a result, such categories are nearly meaningless. And yet the financial world churns out stuff like the Bloomberg piece every day. They are silly and a waste of time. What is "value" (or "growth") but some arbitrary definition?

One of the more amusing examples I've seen of meaningless categories involves Exxon Mobil. Steven Bregman of Horizon Kinetics, a New York-based money management firm, pointed out that Exxon Mobil can be found in almost any ETF. In a presentation titled "Indexation: Capitalist Tool (Delivery agent of The Great Bubble)," delivered at Grant's conference in October 2016, he said:

> Aside from being 25% of the iShares U.S. Energy ETF, 22% of the Vanguard Energy ETF, and so forth, Exxon is simultaneously a Dividend Growth stock and a Deep Value stock. It is in the USA Quality Factor ETF and in the Weak Dollar U.S. Equity ETF. Get this: It's both a Momentum Tilt stock and a Low Volatility stock. It sounds like a vaudeville act.

See the nearby table "Exxon Mobil: It's Growth, It's Value, It's a Bird, It's a Plane..." Knowing this, who cares what the MSCI USA Value Index did relative to the MSCI USA Growth Index? It is ridiculous on the face of it.

Yet, many investors take this kind of "analysis" very seriously. I know asset allocators and investment advisors who will make decisions on where to invest based on this kind of thinking.

Exxon Mobil: It's Growth, It's Value, It's a Bird, It's a Plane...

It's Exxon, a Stock for Every Strategy:	
QUAL	iShares USA Quality Factor ETF
DGRO	iShares Core Dividend Growth ETF
HDV	iShares Core High Dividend ETF
IWD	iShares Russell 1000 Value ETF
EXT	WisdomTree Total Earnings ETF
PBP	Powershares S&P 500 **BuyWrite** ETF
TILT	FlexShares Morningstar US Market Factors Tilt ETF
QUS	SPDR MSCI USA StrategicFactors ETF
GSLC	Goldman Sachs **ActiveBeta** US Large Cap Equity ETF
JHML	John Hancock Multifactor Large Cap ETF
TOK	iShares MSCI Kokusai ETF
ACWI	iShares MSCI ACWI ETF
MMTM	SPDR S&P 1500 **Momentum** Tilt ETF
DVP	**Deep Value** ETF
USWD	WisdomTree **Weak Dollar** US Equity ETF

They'll allocate more toward "value" or "growth" depending on which category seems to be doing better at the moment or seems to have better prospects. They treat these categories as if they were real, subjecting them to statistical analysis and trying to predict which will outperform the other.

If you want to get on the path to clear thinking, you have to see through this charade of "value" versus "growth" – and all of its many manifestations, multiplied across many verbal and conceptual siblings and cousins. You have to recognize it as arbitrary and made up and nonexistent in the real world.

In fact, even the idea of "stocks" is something that exists only in our heads. Nobody owns "stocks." And there is no such thing as a "stock market." What people own is Exxon Mobil (XOM), or Apple (AAPL), or Facebook (FB). They own individual companies (or funds). And those individual companies (and funds) are all different.

Just think about it. If you took a list of the top 10 best-performing S&P 500 stocks in 2016 and compared it with a list of the 10 worst-performing stocks, you would see a huge disparity in returns. (See the nearby table "The best and worst S&P 500 stock performers for 2016.")

The Best and Worst S&P 500 Stock Performers for 2016

The Best		The Worst	
1.	Nvidia, up 224%	1.	Endo International, down 73%
2.	Oneok, up 133%	3.	First Solar, down 51%
4.	Freeport-McMoRan, up 95%	5.	TripAdvisor, down 46%
6.	Newmont Mining, up 89%	7.	Perrigo, down 42%
8.	Applied Materials, up 73%	9.	Vertex Pharmaceuticals, down 41%

Source: "Wall Street in 2016: The best and worst S&P 500 stock performers for 2016" by Angelo Young, *Salon*, December 31, 2016.

It's empirically true that all stocks are not the same. To assert otherwise is to assert something that is false to the facts.

But I hear people talk as if stocks were all the same. People say, "Stocks are expensive," or "Stocks are going to go up," or "Stocks are going to go down." And they'll engage in serious discussion about it – with charts and facts and jibber-jabber about interest rates and the economy and the Fed, etc. But they're talking about an abstraction – something that doesn't exist in a practical sense.

(Now, you can keep going with this and say that even Facebook doesn't really exist as a physical thing. And if so, you are getting ahead of me. We will say more about this later...)

You might say, "Well, true stocks are all different. But many of them do seem to move together." And if you did think that, you are already on a path to clearer thinking. At least here, you've acknowledged "many" is not "all." And "seem to" is not "is." Even so, you've got work to do. By the time you finish this book, you'll see why.

Let's go through another example from the easier side of the spectrum.

In real estate, there is a system of classification for buildings. There are three types of buildings: Class A, Class B, and Class C. The first category of buildings will include those

How Do You Know?

that have the highest rents in their area. They are considered among the finest and most desirable properties. Class B buildings are one step down from that. And Class C buildings are yet one step further down from Class B.

There is more to it than I'm letting on here, but the important thing to know is that these classes are definitions we create and then tag on buildings. Abracadabra, we create with words. But we have to realize that such tags are not part of those buildings in any real sense.

Naming something does not tell us much about the thing so named. As a society we way overstate the power of a name. I always think of the story told by Richard Feynman:

> "See that bird?" he says. "It's a Spencer's warbler. ... Well, in Italian, it's a Chutto Lapittida. In Portuguese, it's a Bom da Peida. In Chinese, it's a Chung-long-tah, and in Japanese, it's a Katano Tekeda. You can know the name of that bird in all the languages of the world, but when you're finished, you'll know absolutely nothing whatever about the bird. You'll only know about humans in different places, and what they call the bird. So let's look at the bird and see what it's doing—that's what counts." (I learned very early the difference between knowing the name of something and knowing something.)

When we call a stock a "value stock," "growth stock," "cyclical stock," or whatever, we should not assume we know anything about that particular stock. We know only what other people call it. (I'll have more on this when we talk about how you should not trust labels.) Focus instead on what the thing does, how it behaves, etc.

So, back to the Class A, B, and C buildings: An investor I know was busy at work making the case that Class A malls were a good place to invest as compared to B or C malls. He believed the A malls had inherent superior characteristics. They were "unique" and "always in demand."

I would not to get too enamored with the definitions. Buildings that are Class A today may be Class B tomorrow, or even Class C – and vice versa. I asked him, "How many Class B or Class C malls today were once Class A?"

All you can say is that you have buildings people call Class A today, based on a definition. That's not saying much. Investors are mostly concerned with what kind of return they are going to get. Besides, so far as I know, there is not a strong correlation between returns and building classes. Just because you own a Class A building doesn't mean you're going to get the highest return. In fact, there may be a loose correlation, but it runs the opposite way. That is, the Class C buildings at the bottom of the quality spectrum as a class tend to do better. (Even if this were true, I'd be suspicious; we'll get to why you should distrust such correlations later in the book.)

But the point is: Here we have a professional investor committing clients' money to an idea based largely around the thesis that one definitional category (Class A) is better than another definitional category. But in reality, once again, there are no Class A buildings or any other classes in the real world. There are only different buildings with broadly similar characteristics.

I would ignore the designations of Class A and such, and instead focus on the financial characteristics of the buildings themselves. Focus on how they actually perform, on the price you'd pay to own them relative to the potential return, and risk of loss, not on what label people agree to place on the assets today.

Once again, clear thinking means looking past a definition. It means seeing through this abstraction of building categories. Don't think because you own "Class A buildings" that this tag, "Class A," is affixed to or somehow inherent in the physical thing. It is not.

Broadly speaking, the two aspects of magical thinking above fall in the category of the magical power of a definition. We love definitions. We fight endlessly over what is what. It's nonsense. Just because you can create definitions and pin them on things doesn't mean they have any validity. And yet, it sometimes seems to me, the bulk of differences, arguments, and discussions is really over definitions.

This morning as I write this, I see a post from an investor titled "Is it a Tool or a Platform?" The entire post is an attempt to solve a self-created problem! "One of the toughest things about analyzing companies is figuring out if they are tools or platforms," the author writes. "It's pretty critical that we figure out the difference."

Why? "Tools" and "platforms" are just words. Forget about them. Focus on what the companies do and less on what they're called or how they're defined. Once you see this madness, you will start to see it everywhere. (In the same morning, I saw an article titled "Is economics a science?" Again, we find an entire column fussing over a definition. I'm telling you, it's everywhere.)

I want to give you a more challenging example of magical thinking to show you once this kind of thinking soaks into in your bones, it can lead you down radical (and liberating) paths.

Yes, You Can Change History

You have surely heard people say, "You can't change history."

Of course you can.

The thinking error here comes from the misconception that history is a series of events existing as a reality separate from how we think about them. Not so. History exists only as interpretation, as memory, as stories we tell ourselves. All of which we can, and do, change.

I want to share an interesting passage on this from the philosopher Oliver Reiser (from *Logic and General Semantics: Writings of Oliver L. Reiser and Others*, edited by Sanford Berman):

> There is a very general belief that the past is irrevocable, that history cannot be changed. Now, it is doubtless true that the past is past, but certainly this does not prove that the past is unalterable. ... In the cultural interpretation of human history, the past is what it is because of its influence on the present. And if we change the present, we have in a sense altered the past. ... If, in the sphere of individual history, the meaning of an experience suddenly breaks upon us, that original event is no longer what it was. **Experiences and events are what they function as, and if we change the effects and meanings, these original phenomena are no longer what they were, at least to us.** There is here a real alchemy in events that is grounded in time's living progress. [Bold added].

This alchemical magic is why there are new interpretations of the American Revolution every generation or new biographies of Abraham Lincoln and on and on. It is because each historian can re-write the story by casting new meanings and tracing different effects onto selected past experiences and events. The historian, in a way, fuses "thinking-feeling about the present" with "what has gone on before."

It is perfectly legitimate to do so. As we will learn later, reality is a product of the observer and the observed. There is no such thing as objectivity. To be objective is like trying to bite your own ear. It can't be done. Everything we "see" must be processed and filtered through our human nervous system. And no two people process and filter in the same way.

To cast the same idea of "history as only what we think of it" in more poetic terms, I want to share this passage from Alan Watts' autobiography, *In My Own Way*: "The past is nothing but a present memory, a shadow, a trace; the illusion that a cigarette whirled in the dark is an actual circle of fire." (Watts wrote beautiful, philosophical books and is most famous as a popularizer of "Eastern religions." We'll come back to his ideas and insights throughout this book.)

What is history? It is words and symbols. Abracadabra again. We create history with words.

Let us look at one more example before we move on. It is another one of my favorites for its initial shock value.

1 + 1 Does Not Always Equal 2

You probably take for granted that $1 + 1 = 2$. It's often thrown about as if it were some kind of law that is true always and everywhere. And yet it isn't.

The statement "$1 + 1 = 2$" is a statement made up of symbols. They are not real-world phenomena. In the real world, many things are not additive. Alfred Korzybski, an important thinker that we will hear more from in the next chapter, wrote in his magnum opus, *Science and Sanity*:

In chemistry, for instance, does hydrogen 'plus' oxygen produce water, H2O? If we mix the two gases, two parts of hydrogen with one of oxygen we do not get water. We must first pass a spark through the mixture, when an explosion occurs and the result becomes *water*, a *new* compound quite *different* from its elements or from a mere mixture of them. Does one gallon of water and one gallon of alcohol make two gallons of a mixture? No, it makes less than two gallons. Does light added to light make more light? Not always. The phenomena of interference show clearly that light 'added' to light sometimes makes darkness. Four atoms of hydrogen, of atomic weight 1.008, produce, under proper conditions, one atom of helium, not of atomic weight 4.032, but of atomic weight 4. The 0.032 has somehow mysteriously vanished. Such examples could be quoted endlessly. **They show unmistakably that structurally this world is not a 'plus' affair, but that *other* than additive principles must be looked for**. [Bold added].

In business and in life, clear thinking requires that we do not assume that $1 + 1$ always equals 2. Often you can combine two things and get something worth much less, as in a merger gone bad. And sometimes you can get something worth much more.

Expecting the real world to obey our made-up equations and mathematical models is a sure path to sloppy thinking and self-deception. That our equations and models seem to often describe how the real world works is a different thing than saying the real world adheres to our equations and models. Markets have a way of humbling, and even ruining, those who think otherwise.

A Warning to You, Reader

I wrote this book because it is a book I *wanted* to write. The ideas herein have been a preoccupation of mine for the last couple of years. I didn't write it for money. In fact, I can pretty much guarantee you that I won't make any money off it.

However, I also wrote this little book with you in mind. By that I mean: I want you to enjoy reading it, whatever else you think of the philosophy I espouse in these pages. There are few things more annoying to me than a writer whose writing is a chore to get through.

In this book I try to get you to think about ideas and concepts in ways you perhaps never thought of them before. I'm offering you a look at a meta-discipline that has not been shared in the investing community since 1958. It's had a big impact on my thinking, and writing this book has helped me sort it all out for myself. These ideas may have a similar impact on you.

But...

The warning I want to give you is that this book will not teach you the nuts and bolts of any particular investing strategy. I'm not vouching for any particular style of investing in what follows. I write from an investing perspective, but in some ways this book is as much about thinking and life as it is about investing.

In the spirit of Charlie Munger's worldly wisdom, I'm sharing a mental model you can add to your own latticework of models.

Munger, who is the famous and wise vice chairman of Warren Buffett's Berkshire Hathaway, said of his first rule of worldly wisdom:

> Well, the first rule is that you've got to have multiple models because if you just have one or two that you're using, the nature of human psychology is such that you'll torture reality so that it fits your models, or at least you'll think it does. ...
>
> And the models have to come from multiple disciplines because all the wisdom of the world is not to be found in one little academic department. That's why poetry professors, by and large, are so unwise in a worldly sense. They don't have enough models in their heads. So you've got to have models across a fair array of disciplines.
>
> You may say, "My God, this is already getting way too tough." But, fortunately, it isn't that tough because 80 or 90 important models will carry about 90% of the freight in making you a worldly wise person. And, of those, only a mere handful really carry very heavy freight.

I believe the model offered here can carry a lot of very heavy freight.

With that, we begin our journey through the mind-bending, magical world of our abstractions. In Part I, "Ways of Knowing," we'll look at what general semantics is all about and what it teaches us about the limits of our knowledge. In Part II, "Devices for Clear Thinking," we'll look at various tricks and tools to help clarify your thinking. And in Part III, "Chapel Perilous," we'll tie it all together and reach some bold conclusions.

Key Takeaways

- Our understanding of Wall Street, investing, and life rests on words and symbols, which are not the things they aim to represent.

- This book will help you see through these abstractions. For example, you should not rely on terms such as "value stocks" and "growth stocks." There are no "value stocks" or "growth stocks." These terms rest on varying and arbitrary definitions created by people.

- Stocks are not all the same, as any table of the best- and worst-performing stocks in any given year (or series of years) will show. Yet we often talk about "stocks" as if they were all the same. For example, "Stocks are expensive (or cheap)."

- The phrase, "you can't change history" rests on a faulty assumption that there is an objective view of past events. You can change history because history is our interpretation of what has gone before. As philosopher Oliver Reiser put it, "Experiences and events are what they function as, and if we change the effects and meanings, these original phenomena are no longer what they were, at least to us."

- 1 + 1 does not always equal 2. For example, 1 gallon of water plus 1 gallon of alcohol is not 2 gallons of mixture but something less. This, and many other examples, shows you that the world is not an additive affair.

- This book will teach you the basics of a meta-discipline that has not been shared with Wall Street since 1958.

Part I

Ways of Knowing

Chapter 1

The Map and the Mapmaker

"The map is not the territory."

~ Alfred Korzybski (1879-1950)

We'll begin with Alfred Korzybski, whose ideas figure prominently in our story. His most famous metaphor helps set the purpose (and usefulness) of our project. We'll take a look at a few of his key contributions and how they help us see the limitations of our abstractions. His ideas form the building blocks for our approach.

Korzybski was born in Poland, fought in WWI with the Russian army, and moved to the US after the war (after a stint in Canada). As a young man he studied engineering, but his future lay as a hard-working independent scholar in a field of his own making.

Korzybski wrote the seminal text on a new meta-discipline he called "general semantics." Published in 1933, *Science and Sanity: An Introduction to Non-Aristotelian Systems and General Semantics* took him 12 years to write. He relied on material from a wide range of disciplines – anthropology, biology, chemistry, epistemology, history, logic, mathematics, neurology, physics, psychiatry, and much more. It is a big, fat, hard-to-read book. Bound in a blue hardcover, students dubbed it "the blue peril."

(It repays study, I can tell you. But I wouldn't start with *S&S*. See the bibliographic essay at the end of this book for a suggested course of study if you want to pursue these ideas further.)

The book sold well and attracted some attention in academic circles, garnering warm endorsements from leading scientists in a variety of fields. Korzybski's work attracted a following among many capable and intelligent thinkers, some of who would go on to write their own books on the subject. And general semantics flourished over the next two decades.

Korzybski's name and ideas are not well-known today. You probably had not heard of him before picking up this book. But you probably had heard the phrase most often associated with him: "The map is not the territory."

How Do You Know?

Think about a map of, say, the United States. The map is an abstraction. It may include states and capitals and show rivers and borders. But it also leaves a lot of things out. Seeing "New York City" on a map is quite a different thing than standing in the middle of Times Square on New Year's Eve.

In general semantics, maps stand as a powerful metaphor for our ideas, concepts, definitions, theories, etc. Korzybski stressed that the usefulness of a map was in its similarity to the territory it supposedly mapped. Maps can be "wrong."

For example, what if you saw a map that had New York between Chicago and San Francisco? You'd say that's absurd. Geographically, you know San Francisco is west of New York City, and New York City is east of Chicago.

You could say, then, this strange map does not reflect the territory it supposedly represents. New York is not between Chicago and San Francisco. Korzybski would resist calling it a "bad" map, because he felt doing so did not give you an important conclusion. What does "bad" mean exactly? "We use moral terms, 'bad,' 'wrong,' 'false,' etc., and nothing of importance follows," he said in his *General Semantics Seminar 1937*. "Do we get any wisdom out of such statements? No."

This seems as good a place as any to share how Korzybski used single quotation marks. In addition to standard usage, he used them as a way to flag a suspect term such as 'bad.' In finance, we have lots of suspect terms, such as 'stock market,' 'profits,' 'the economy,' and 'GDP.' We'll see more why these are suspect as we go deeper into the text.

Henceforth, in this book, I will also follow Korzybski's convention, as outlined in the *General Semantics Bulletin*: "to mark off terms and phrases which seem to varying degrees questionable for neurolinguistic, neurophysiological, methodological, or general epistemological reasons." I won't be dogmatic about it and sprinkle single quotes everywhere, but I will use it judiciously to highlight terms where you should exercise particular care in handling them.

Korzybski, as you might gather, was a stickler for a high level of linguistic clarity (to which I aspire but surely fall short). So Korzybski – instead of calling a map 'good' or 'bad' – thought of maps in terms of whether they were *similar in structure* to the territory or not.

In the example above, our map was not similar in structure to the territory. It was false-to-facts. Following this map would have led us astray. Likewise, when our abstractions – those ideas, concepts, theories, definitions, etc. – do not match the territory, we fall into error. As Korzybski said, "for maximum probability of maximum predictability we must have a map similar in structure to the territory."

For example, most people are surprised to learn that Australia is more than three times as large as Greenland because they are used to seeing maps where Greenland appears so large. But these maps are not similar in structure to the territory they represent. Trying to make a flat representation of a globe leads to problems of distortion. (See the website https://thetruesize.com for more fun geographical surprises.)

Similar in structure does not mean simply an accurate representation, however. The aforementioned Francis Chisholm says it is best to understand the concept through the use of examples rather than trying to pin down a definition:

> Two things can be similar in structure although completely different in material. There is a similarity in structure between the grooves in a phonograph record and the music that is played from it. There is a similarity in structure between a blueprint and a machine it is made from.

Chessboards of all different sizes and materials have a similarity in structure among them. The same play performed on different nights by different actors still has a similarity in structure between them. Similarity in structure depends on order and relationships that exist in both things being compared.

This was an important discovery, one that set Korzybski's effort apart from prevailing orientations. Gad Horowitz, a teacher of general semantics, wrote an excellent book titled *The Book of Radical General Semantics*. In it, he called the notion of similarity-in-structure "a master stroke without which the understanding of General Semantics risks sliding back to the Aristotelian orientation."

Aristotelian vs. Non-Aristotelian

I should say something here about that odd term "Aristotelian." You may recall from above that Korzybski chose as the subtitle for his opus "an introduction to non-Aristotelian systems and general semantics." A discussion on Aristotelian and non-Aristotelian systems can get us into some deep waters. I will only skim the surface.

Aristotle, I'm sure, needs no introduction. Aristotelian, in this context, primarily refers to a kind of thinking associated with his philosophy. A brief sketch of a few specifics will help frame what Korzybski reacted against and help you see the radical nature of general semantics.

The first is the law of Identity. A is A. Things are what they are. An apple is an apple. That's Aristotelian thinking. A non-A orientation would say, "No, this apple is different from other apples. And every apple is different in countless ways from every other apple." You can have two fresh apples, but they differ in shape, size and color.

These are both apples… yet they are not the same.

Apples as a class have many similarities, but a non-A thinker is alive to the differences, at least as much as the similarities. Of course, the law of identity seems trivial when we're talking about apples.

But it doesn't seem so trivial if we say, "stocks are expensive" (implying all stocks are the same and all stocks are expensive), thereby causing us to miss out on a stock just about to march up tenfold. Or if we think, "All lawyers are the same," and then misjudge a lawyer who is quite different from our experience to that point. Or if we say, "CEOs are liars," and then overlook a key insight from a CEO who wasn't lying. The examples are endless.

And it can be much more grave if we say "A Muslim is a Muslim" or "A Jew is a Jew," implying a sameness that doesn't exist. Some awful ideas and actions begin with such thinking. A non-A orientation would appreciate that all Muslims, for example, are not the same. They are all different in countless ways, as all people are everywhere.

Another point of Aristotelian logic is that A is either A or not-A. This is the law of the excluded middle. A is either an apple or an orange. Closely related to this is the law of non-contradiction. A cannot be both A and not-A.

But a non-A orientation realizes that in the world "out there," most things do not fall into either/or categories. You can be both a father and a son. Something can be both a food and a poison – depending on the amount consumed. A non-A orientation guards against thinking in either/or terms. 'Success' or 'failure,' for example, admits little possibility of a more nuanced outcome. Ditto the idea that you are either a 'winner' or 'loser,' or such murky terms as 'happiness' or 'wealth' or 'cause' and 'effect.'

Bruce Kodish, a general semanticist and Korzybski's biographer, sums up Aristotelian thinking in his book *Drive Yourself Sane*:

> In sum, following the Aristotelian orientation leads us to view the world as static and unchanging. It leads us to assume we can know all. It leads us to assume our categories exist in the world and cannot be changed. It leads us to look for single causes for events. It leads us to evaluate in either/or terms. It leads us to a lack of awareness of our evaluating process. This orientation so permeates our culture that these ways of evaluating still, for most people, seem like common sense.

"Common sense" of the kind Kodish refers to can lead us astray in the swirling, ever-changing, and complex world we live in. A non-A orientation is what this book is all about. A non-A orientation pushes back against Aristotelian assumptions.

General semantics is a non-A system, but it is not the only one. A partial list of other approaches also considered non-A, from the New York Society for General Semantics:

- Alfred North Whitehead and Bertrand Russell's Theory of Logical Types
- Ludwig Wittgenstein's Philosophy of Language
- Susanne Langer's Philosophy of Symbolic Form
- Charles Peirce's Semiotics
- Kurt Gödel's Incompleteness Theorem
- Edward Sapir and Benjamin Lee Whorf's Linguistic Relativism
- G.H. Mead's Symbolic Interactionism
- Charles Kay Ogden and I.A. Richards' Meaning of Meaning
- Albert Einstein's Theory of Relativity
- Werner Heisenberg's Uncertainty Principle
- Claude Shannon's Information Theory
- Norbert Wiener's Cybernetics
- Gregory Bateson's Ecology of Mind
- Ludwig von Bertalanffy's General System Theory
- Paul Watzlawick's Relational Communication
- Kenneth Burke's Dramatistic Rhetoric
- Erving Goffman's Dramaturgical Sociology
- Edward T. Hall and Ray Birdwhistell's Nonverbal Communication
- Lev Vygotsky and Alexander Luria's Cultural Historical Psychology
- George Lakoff and Mark Johnson's Metaphor Theory
- Marshall McLuhan and Neil Postman's Media Ecology

This list provides quite an interesting program for self-study. Later in the book, we'll touch on one of these non-A systems, that of Sapir and Whorf.

A non-A orientation is equivalent to a non-Euclidean geometry or a non-Newtonian (i.e., quantum) physics. It upends age-old assumptions and infuses newer scientific thinking in its place.

A non-A orientation realizes that whatever map (idea, concept, theory, etc.) we use, that map is not the territory. Our maps are reproductions of certain chosen details. They are representations, but they can never be the things they represent.

A photo of a savory barbeque can never be the barbeque itself; no matter how good a representation, you can never taste it.

The philosopher Alan Watts put it another way: "The menu is not the meal." The words you read on the page of a menu are not the meal itself. Or as another philosopher, Jiddu Krishnamurti, said in *Think on These Things*, "A symbol, a word, is not the thing it represents. The word 'door' is not the door, is it?"

I know this seems obvious, but again, we often forget and fog up our thinking as a result of forgetting. We assume 'Class A building' is a physical thing that exists. When we describe something using a word, we often think somehow we've captured what it is. A non-A orientation rejects this.

Maps Leave Things Out

There are many other implications: If the map is not the territory, then the map is not all of the territory. In other words, we always leave details out. Whatever we say, think, etc., we leave something out. What we leave out could be important.

Maps are also self-reflexive. Meaning, we can make a map of the map. And we can make a map of the map of the map. Put another way, we can create abstractions based on our abstractions. We can make theories about our theories. We can have concepts built on concepts.

The existence of maps, too, implies the existence of a mapmaker. And that mapmaker is a human being with a nervous system that filtered and made sense of the world around him or her. No two nervous systems see the world in exactly the same way. They bring different experiences, different temperaments, different biases, etc.

The idea of maps as explained by Korzybski helps us be conscious of our abstractions and their limitations. We can't help but make maps and abstract from the world around us. It's the way we make sense of things. However, we should know when we do it and how it places limits on what we really know.

If we aim for clarity of thought, as we set out in the beginning, then consciousness of abstracting is a critical skill to learn. I would say that consciousness of abstracting is a big part of what Korzybski's whole project is all about. But K's general semantics is about so much more.

Korzybski spent over 800 pages, and used a lot of math and footnotes, to describe his new meta-discipline in *Science and Sanity*. So whatever I say here can only diminish the scope of his achievement. (I can only make a map of his map.) In a way, the book in your hands is a distillation and restatement of *some* of the principles of *Science and Sanity* applied to investing. I owe a large debt to Korzybski in any case.

To backtrack a bit: Before *Science and Sanity*, Korzybski published another book in 1921 called *Manhood of Humanity*, in which he introduced his concept of "time-binding." Robert Pula, a longtime teacher of general semantics, called time-binding (in his invaluable *A General-Semantics Glossary*) "another 'given' of general-semantics, an underlying formulation and commitment out of which the rest of the system grows."

To be brief about it, time-binding is what distinguishes mankind from other animals. ("Some people, Disney-bred anthropomorphists, don't like this," Pula says, heading off an objection. "They see it as 'putting down' our wee beastie brothers and sisters. When I see a dog- or dolphin-built library, I'll reconsider the issue.") It is the ability to transmit knowledge and experience across generations. It is our capacity to tap into the labors and experiences of the past, to share what we have learned with future time-binders. It is a fundamental building block of our civilization.

Korzybski described human beings by what they do. And he emphasized that our use of symbols is what facilitates time-binding. Language (and symbols, more broadly), then, becomes a crucial matter. As Pula says: "Thus general-semantics as a systematic description-cum-diagnosis of verbal/nonverbal relationships and a method to promote proper evaluating, i.e., successful time-binding."

Korzybski's Structural Differential

Now, I'd like to introduce Korzybski's famous structural differential. This strange-looking model helps show us how abstracting works. It illustrates the idea of "the map is not the territory." The model makes clear the obvious limitations of our maps.

In Kodish's biography of Korzybski, he gives the backstory on the creation of the structural differential. Korzybski came up with it during a talk in 1923 where he sketched out the diagram off-hand to make a point.

Korzybski's Structual Differential

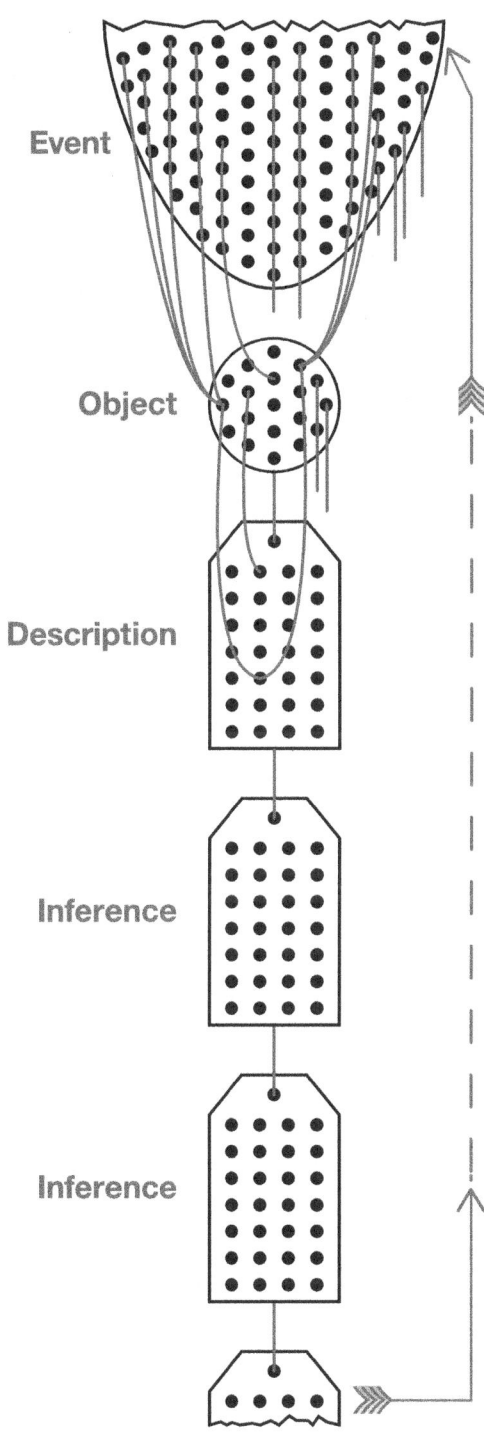

Later he came to think it was a great breakthrough and that it captured what he was trying to get people to understand. (Still the engineer at heart, he apparently fashioned nice-looking models made of wood in his workshop. I keep thinking I'd like to make one to hang in my office. It would make a great conversation piece, besides serving as a reminder to be conscious of my own abstractions.)

So what is this model with the mysterious name of "structural differential"? Take a look at the nearby diagram. It needs explaining.

The "Event" level is the world out there; process may be a better word than event as it represents an ever-changing mosaic of happenings. All those dots and strings are the possible details that you could pick up through your human nervous system. The jagged line at the top of the parabola shows that there are a seemingly infinite number of details about the world out there that you cannot perceive.

Let's imagine we're sitting in a park. The "Event" level is everything that is going on around us, whether we're aware of it or not. It is every detail – every blade of grass, a bird in a tree, a sound, a smell, etc. Even things beyond our ability to detect, such as radio waves, infrared light, etc. Everything.

The "Object" level comes next. It shows your perceptions of that "Event." It represents the details you pick up.

So again, think back to us sitting in a park. You're aware of the dog running in the grass. You see a few trees. You hear a bird sing. You're aware of the park bench you're sitting on. These are things you pick up, the dots and strings on the "Object" level.

But... as the diagram shows, you don't pick up all the dots and all the strings. Some of the strings don't connect from the "Event" to the "Object." There are fewer dots on the "Object" than the "Event." This shows you that some things are left out. You cannot possibly process all the details of the "Event." You don't pick up every bug, bird, leaf, blade of grass, sound, smell, etc.

In short, the "Object" level is what you immediately perceive at the nonverbal level – it is your first impressions, visual images, feelings, tastes, textures, etc.

The next level is "Description." This is where you first start to conceptualize and put things into words. This is your making of the map. The important thing here is again the leaving out of details. You cannot put all of what you experience into words. You must again abstract; you must leave things out. And that is reflected in the diagram as more dots and strings fall behind and the "Description" itself takes on a shape different from the Object and Event levels.

So, we're sitting in the park, and you see someone run by. There's the "Event" – a swirl of happenings and details of which you grasp only a fraction (the "Object" level). From the Object level you see someone in running shorts and shoes, T-shirt sweated through (the "Description"). The Object level you might think of as the focus of your attention. In this case, the runner.

And now you are in a position to draw your first "Inference."

This Inference level is where you start to draw meaning from that map you made. And then you can draw further inferences from that inference. The jagged edge at the end of the last inference is meant to show that there is no end to the amount of inferences you can draw. The arrow that leads back to the Event level shows how your inferences then impact what you "see" at the Event level. There is an ongoing feedback loop of happenings and thinking-feeling.

Back to the park and person who just ran by us. Your first inference might be: "This person is jogging through the park." A second inference might be: "This person must be in good shape." And so on…

But your inferences could be wrong. Maybe you didn't see the woman waiving her arms and chasing him. The runner is actually a purse-snatcher and is making a getaway.

In brief, that's how the structural differential works. It is a simple model of the abstracting process. But the implications are profound.

Let's think about an example from investing. The Event level is everything "out there." From that we draw an Object: General Electric.

We want to study this company. General Electric is a huge enterprise. In 2016, it did $123 billion in sales. The company has a dozen subsidiaries and employs 330,000 people who work all over the world. There is a huge amount of detail you could amass on General Electric, just on the Description level. And our Description can't capture it all.

From this Description we start to draw Inferences. We say it's profitable or it's growing. At some point in our chain of inferences we may conclude the "stock is cheap."

But look how far from the "Event" we've come! Look at all the details we've left out. It makes you quite humble about the value of your inferences. There is so much you can't possibly capture – so much you miss. Possibly, these missing strings and dots are important.

Maybe you left out General Electric's gaping pension deficit, which will eat into future earnings. Maybe your analysis also missed the adjustments GE made to disguise weaknesses in its earnings report. And so again, your inference would be wrong because the details you left out were ones that mattered. The stock dropped nearly 30% in 2017, a loss you may have avoided with a better inference.

I realize the irony in talking about a model about the abstracting process. We shouldn't take the model too literally. There are no levels in the real world. What the model represents can happen in mere seconds, or it may take weeks of work. Even so, the structural differential is quite robust.

More Ways of Thinking About the Structural Differential

Horowitz, for example, showed off a structural differential made by one of his students. This is hard to show here, but imagine the model as a physical thing. The Event is a bag, the Object is a ball connected to it with string, and then the Description and Inference tags follow, connected like a chain.

In this model, you can take the "Object," "Description," and "Inference" tags and put them inside the bag that is the parabola (or "Event"). Why is this a noteworthy way of presenting the model?

Because it shows you that the tags (Object, Description, Inferences) inhere in what is going on. They don't exist independently on their own. (General Electric, for example, does not exist in a vacuum. It is a process that is part of everything else that is happening "out there.")

In this variation, the "togetherness of the levels can be seen and felt," as Horowitz says:

> I had been emphasizing to the students that although these levels are separate in space in the structural differential, as it is commonly represented, in fact the levels are not separate. Also, the levels are hierarchically structured. The event level contains the object level, even though the object is abstracted from the event. And although the label levels are abstracted from the object level, the object contains the label levels.

The structural differential is a model, after all. In the real world all these things – Event, Object, Description, Inferences – blend and exist together.

Another variation by Milton Dawes, a general semanticist, shows the effect of the passage of time. Here we see how we're constantly drawing abstractions as time passes, and in Dawes' model you can see how they link. (See the nearby graphic, "The Structural Differential and Time.")

The Structural Differential and Time

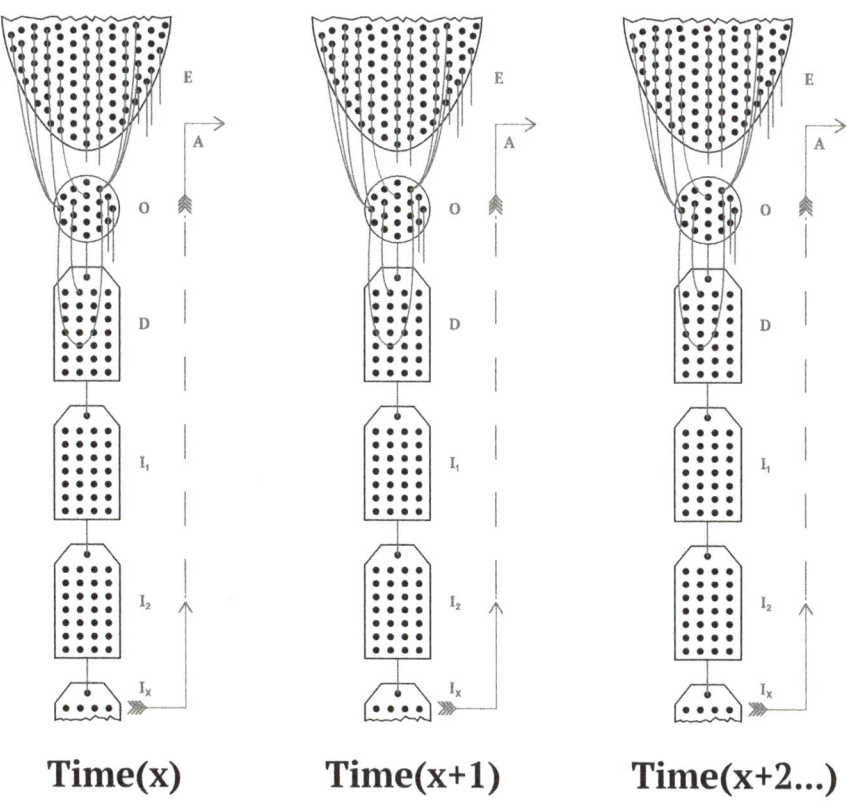

| Time(x) | Time(x+1) | Time(x+2...) |

The idea behind it is simple. Dawes takes the structural differential and puts it in a time series. It captures well the idea that things are constantly changing. The Event is not a static thing, but a process. In such a world, it can be dangerous to stick with Inferences as if they were static tags. Inferences and Descriptions must be updated to reflect the changing nature of the Object and Event levels. (Your description of General Electric might be reasonably accurate today, but it might not be tomorrow after the sale of a division, a new CEO, etc.)

Pula created a similar variation. To see this variant, take Dawes' version and imagine that the "Event" level is one giant parabola (which Pula calls "the plenum") and all the other Object levels start at this single parabola. I like this variation too because it gives prominence to the idea that the plenum is a giant, ever-changing process from which we constantly draw our abstractions.

In either case, the point of both Dawes and Pula is to capture the idea that we make our abstractions across space-time.

Working with the structural differential helps you develop a sense for your own abstractions. Dawes puts it elegantly in "Using the Structural Differential" (1994):

> If we accept that we don't know 'all' that's going on around us, we're less likely to be close-minded about our ideas, opinions, decisions, etc. … If we accept that we don't know 'all', we are more likely to develop a theoretical, experimental, and less absolutistic approach to what we believe, what we understand or know, and what we do. We adopt a continuous learning approach to living when we are aware that there is more information available to us than what we presently have.

As an investor, learning the lessons embedded in the structural differential will go a long way toward making you more conscious of your own abstracting. Make your own structural differential and hang it on your wall.

One last fascinating tidbit before we leave the structural differential: The model seems quite similar to Einstein's own model of thinking. As Kodish writes in *Dare to Inquire*:

> While Einstein's model emphasizes the scientist's process of making conjectural jumps from experience, applying 'logic,' and then testing against experience, the

structural differential emphasizes the structure of the underlying neuro-psychological process of abstracting through which this takes place.

Perhaps that will nudge you to give the structural differential a deeper look. I know "structural differential" is a funny name and that it looks strange. It may seem off-putting and even silly, but I would simply urge you to try it. Play with the model and apply it.

Korzybski's work has been enriched by the work of many able thinkers over the decades. The more time I've spent with his material, the more I've come to respect and admire his achievements. I've come to find him an inspiring figure. He seems like he was a hard-working and decent man, who wanted to help others think through and solve their problems.

Korzybski was an independent scholar. He had no tenured position or salary from a university. He often struggled to find the money to keep his work going and his fledgling Institute of General Semantics – which he founded in 1938 – financially afloat. But he kept at it, aided by some remarkably capable people who shared his vision and dedication.

Kodish, his biographer, called Korzybski an "epistemological knight-errant," which is a nice way to think about him, wandering over the intellectual landscape of humanity and gently removing our illusions.

So, we have a foundation. Let's chase down its many applications and implications.

Key Takeaways

- Alfred Korzybski (1879-1950) was the intellectual pioneer who created the meta-discipline of general semantics, which is largely the focus of this book. I owe a great debt to Korzybski.

- Korzybski coined the phrase "the map is not the territory." Maps stand for our ideas, concepts, theories, etc. These maps are only useful insofar as they share a *similarity in structure* with the reality they represent.

- There are at least a few powerful implications from Korzybski's analogy, including the idea that maps always leave things out. And what they leave out could be important.

- We introduced the idea of time-binding, which is mankind's ability to transmit knowledge and experience across generations. This is a "given" in general semantics, and the rest of the system grows from it.

- In this chapter, we discussed the essential differences between Aristotelian- and non-Aristotelian systems. General semantics is a non-A orientation. Among other things, a non-A orientation realizes that in the world "out there," most things do not fall into either/or categories.

- The "structural differential" is Korzybski's model of the abstracting process. It is a robust model that shows how we leave details out when we make inferences from what happens "out there." Use it and internalize what it teaches.

Chapter 2

Distrust Cause-and-Effect Type Thinking

"History has chance after chance to prove men fools."

~ Charles Bukowski (1920-1994), poet, *The Roominghouse Madrigals*

One thing you may begin to appreciate after playing with Korzybski's ideas for a bit is the complexity of the world around us. Making good inferences, then, becomes a tricky matter.

Take the simple idea of cause and effect, which is an inference. In this chapter, we'll explore why drawing cause and effect relationships is much more difficult than you might think – perhaps even impossible.

Yet, the way many people talk about cause and effect often reflects a lack of appreciation for the utter complexities of markets and life.

Consider the following:

- "When interest rates rise, stocks will fall."

- "Lower taxes will cause stock prices to rise."

- "High debt levels mean lower growth."

- "Higher growth means stocks will rise."

First, you'll note the heavy abstractions: 'interest rates,' 'stocks,' 'lower taxes,' 'debt levels,' 'growth.' These words, as we've seen, beg many questions. (Which stocks? What taxes? Which debts? 'High' compared to what? 'Lower' by how much? Etc.)

Even looking past the abstractions, you should distrust simple cause-and-effect explanations such as these – no matter the proof offered. You'll see why below.

Remember when people used to say that when quantitative easing (QE) ended, the 'stock market' would tank? Beginning in 2008, the Federal Reserve Bank bought 'bonds' (QE) to drive 'interest rates' lower.

Well, if you plotted the Fed's QE program against the S&P 500 Index ('the stock market'), you saw a nice clean correlation. Ergo, it appeared that QE propped up the market. That chart got a lot of play, even from apparently intelligent people.

But QE ended in 2014. And the market kept rolling. Just two years later, the market put in a new all-time high. So much for that!

The error people made in thinking QE propped up the market was in mistaking correlation for causation. But correlation is not causation, as your statistics teacher surely used to teach you. (The second mistake is thinking that any single factor drives 'the market.')

You may remember the old joke about the man on the street corner waving a red flag. Finally, someone goes up to him and asks what he's doing. "I'm keeping the elephants away." "But there are no elephants here." "Then it's working." Right.

One of my favorite examples of correlation analysis gone awry comes from David Leinweber at Caltech who wrote a paper in 1995 called "Stupid Data Miner Tricks: Overfitting the S&P 500."

He showed that butter production and the sheep population in Bangladesh, along with U.S. cheese production, "explained" 99% of the movements of the S&P 500 between 1983 and 1993. In other words, if you knew what butter production was in Bangladesh along with its sheep population and U.S. cheese production, you could predict where the S&P 500 would go.

Leinweber used regression analysis, which is the statistical technique that people use to produce this kind of analysis. But Leinweber's was an obvious parody. He was making fun of a type of thinking that is all too common. His was a blatant example of why you should distrust such analysis.

And yet we still see it everywhere. The financial world pumps out nonsense like the Bangladesh example every day. But the nonsense usually is not so obvious. It is subtle. The correlations plotted seem plausible. But as Leinweber warns us, "Just because something appears plausible, it doesn't mean that it is."

(If you want to have some fun drawing up spurious correlations, see the webpage "Spurious Correlations" at http://www.tylervigen.com/spurious-correlations. You'll find such classics as how "per capita cheese consumption" correlates with the "number of people who died by becoming tangled in their bedsheets." Yes, there is a stat for that.)

Yet people keep trying.

How Do You Know?

More Data-Mining Exercises, More Futility

The CAPE ratio is another popular metric to gauge the "valuation of the market," but it is another data-mining exercise. CAPE means "cyclically adjusted price-to-earnings," also known as the Shiller P/E. Applied to the U.S. S&P 500 equity market, it is price divided by the average of 10 years of earnings, adjusted for inflation. The contention is that the 'market' mean reverts, and so the Shiller P/E can be used to gauge whether the 'market' is undervalued or overvalued. Basically, if the 'market' P/E is above the Shiller P/E, you'd deduce it's overvalued.

I never understood the popularity of this ratio. The fact that a PhD economist named Robert Shiller promotes its use probably helps. It's amazing what you can get away with in this country if you can get yourself called "doctor." (Apologies to Christopher Hitchens, who once said "you can get away with the most extraordinary offenses to morality and to truth in this country if you'll just get yourself called 'reverend.'") And Shiller has a Nobel Prize – doubly dangerous!

CAPE is an assault on common sense.

Let me count three reasons why, in no particular order of importance: First, it is backward-looking. Let me ask you: When you look at a company today in 2017, do you put any weight on what it earned in 2007? Or 2008? Or 2009? I don't. And I would advise that you don't either. But CAPE does.

The reason you shouldn't is that companies change. Why should I care what, say, Berkshire Hathaway earned in 2006 or 2007? It owns businesses today it didn't even own back then. It's practically a different firm.

This goes for most businesses. They're different now than they were then. Restaurants own more restaurants. Retailers own more stores (or less). Share counts change, especially with buybacks (which reduce shares outstanding). Accounting rules change. The mix of businesses in the index changes too – from heavy manufacturing to service to tech. All have different P/Es. People come and go, including CEOs, CFOs, etc.

Second, mean reversion is a questionable way to look at markets. I know this sounds like heresy. Everybody seems to believe in mean reversion, or the idea that markets revert to an average. But the mean itself constantly changes. Also, which mean do you use? The five-year? Ten-year? Twenty-year? How about 50-year? You get different answers. Your choice is arbitrary.

And mean of what? Does it even make sense to average price-earnings ratios over time? Lots of things impact price-earnings ratios – such as interest rates, expected growth rates, debt levels, and more.

Less obvious, but perhaps most important: There is no rule that says markets have to revert to some average. The concept of an average is just an imaginary construction that exists in our heads. There is no average in real life. It has no physical existence, and it is not a constraint on anything. Our averages are like lines of latitude on the globe; they are just concepts.

CAPE advocates like to say it works, as far as having some predictive value about future equity returns. They should say, "It seems to have worked in the past over the very long run." And that's not a good argument, because you can find whatever you want in the data – as Leinweber's brilliant study shows.

The same thing applies to many popular, even "sacred" ratios. Warren Buffett once said that market cap to GDP was "probably the best single measure of where valuations stand at any given moment." Well, that sealed this metric's popularity, but it's just another phony.

Why should, say, the valuation of the S&P 500 – which gets more than 40% of earnings from outside the U.S. – be constrained by U.S. GDP? It isn't, and it shouldn't. Normally what happens when I tell people this is they agree, and then they continue to use it anyway. People seem to have a desperate need to believe in some kind of cause-and-effect relationship to make sense of the world. Most seem terrified to live with the idea that things just happen for reasons we can't understand.

As I say, the world is a much more confusing and complex place than we give it credit for. Drawing out reliable cause-and-effect relationships that hold firm in financial markets (and life in general) is hard, really hard. Maybe impossible.

Why It's Hard to Be Sure About Causes and Effects

I once heard author Robert Anton Wilson give a talk – on YouTube; he died in 2007 – where he explained an interesting exercise. He said he got it from reading a book by the mystic Aleister Crowley (1875-1947). Crowley said he got it from a monk in Ceylon (now Sri Lanka). The exercise goes like this: You go find a quiet place to sit, and then you trace out all the reasons you are there at that moment doing that exercise.

So, you might start by saying, "I'm here because I read about this exercise in a book. I read the book because a friend of mine recommended it to me at lunch.

Why was I meeting him at lunch that day? Well, because we regularly meet for lunch. Why..."

And you keep going and pushing as far as you can stand to do it. What you come to realize is the role that chance and happenstance play in your life. Everything had to happen just as it happened for you to be sitting there at that moment.

It also begs the question about what "the cause" was. There seem to be so many things that had to happen just the way they happened. Which one is "the cause"? If even seemingly trivial events don't happen as they did, then perhaps where you are now would change completely as a result.

If you push on with this exercise far enough, you'll get to when your parents met. And if you keep going, you'll eventually get to ancestors. There is, as should be obvious, no end to the trail. And so it sort of throws the whole question of "cause" out the window.

The philosopher Alan Watts talked about this "ancient problem of cause and effect. We believe that every thing and every event must have a cause." He showed how the problem comes from not seeing the whole picture. We rely too much on our own chosen set of data points.

He has a most interesting story in *The Book: On the Taboo Against Knowing Who You Are*, which brings home the point:

> Here is someone who has never seen a cat. He is looking through a narrow slit in a fence, and, on the other side, a cat walks by. He sees first the head, then the less distinctly shaped furry trunk, and then the tail. Extraordinary! The cat turns round and walks back, and again he sees the head, and a little later the tail. This sequence begins to look like something regular and reliable. Yet again, the cat turns round, and he witnesses the same regular sequence: first the head, and later the tail. Thereupon he reasons that the event head is the invariable and necessary cause of the event tail, which is the head's effect. This absurd and confusing gobbledygook comes from his failure to see that head and tail go together; they are all one cat.

Remember this when you see analysts pull out one or two data points – price-earnings ratio, or debt to GDP, or whatever – and use it to try to "explain" the market. They are all just looking through a narrow slit in the fence. And those data points are all one cat.

How Do You Know?

As ever, humility and doubt are good guides here.

Whenever you see an "If X then Y" statement, you should distrust it.

For example: *If interest rates rise (fall), then stocks will fall (rise)...*

The problems here are many. First off, in markets you can't change one variable and leave everything else the same. Rates may rise (or fall), but what happens to sales growth? What about profit margins? What about countless other things that also continue to change?

Besides, which stocks? The earnings of brokers, banks, and insurance companies generally rise when rates float higher. We've already seen the weakness in talking about "stocks" as if they were all the same.

If the economy picks up speed, that's good for stocks...

We got the "Trump bump" as the market rallied after the 2016 presidential election, presumably under this belief. But there are a lot of problems with this thinking. The connection between 'economic growth' and stock returns is murky. You can have a fast-growing 'economy' and a lousy 'stock market' (and vice versa).

There are a lot of other variables at work – such as valuations. And again, you must ask, which stocks? Moreover, people throw around the phrase 'the economy' as if it were some big animal in the backyard that we can go out and weigh. It's not as if 'the economy's growth rate' is an objective or readily ascertainable number. It is the product of a lot of assumptions. 'Economic growth' is itself an abstraction many steps removed from the world out there (or the Object, if we use Korzybski's model).

Never be too sure of any prediction, no matter how logical or plausible it seems, based on such simple cause and effect analysis. What we're doing when we search for such causes and effects is looking for patterns. We are pattern-seekers. But that's a risky business.

Let's take one more example. Suppose I show you this string of numbers: 14, 23, 34, 42... and then I ask you to pick the next number in the series. What would your answer be?

I'll give you a minute...

Now, you could try all kinds of plausible ways to do this – to try to figure out the mechanism of how one number "causes" another to appear. There is no single pure-math answer. But in this case, using math in this way will lead you astray from the get-go.

The answer sought is 59.

How's that?

Well, it's the next street level where diagonal Broadway crosses an avenue in New York City. (This example comes from Edward MacNeal's *Mathsemantics: Making Numbers Talk Sense*.)

Trick question, you may protest? No. Real life, I say.

Be Aware of the Complexity of Our World

There are many, many factors at work in the 'real world.' And what goes unappreciated perhaps is not so much that there are many factors, but how great an effect even just a single additional variable can have on changing the equation entirely.

In fact, one memorable way to illustrate this is by using an actual equation. The example is Korzybski's, from *Science and Sanity*. Take a look at the nearby figure, which shows a simple straight line made from three points.

Three Points Make A Simple Line

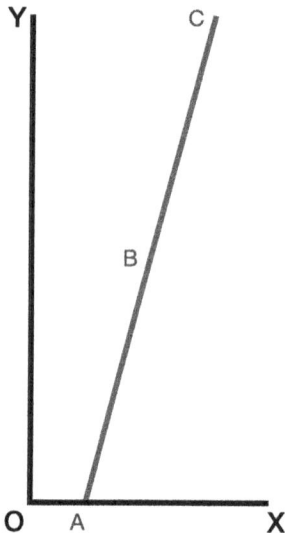

The equation for this line looks like this:

$$Y = 3x - 3$$

Now, what happens when we add one more data point that doesn't fit our previous line? Let's say we add a point at coordinate 2,6. Now look at what happens to our simple line:

Four Points... And Suddenly Not So Simple

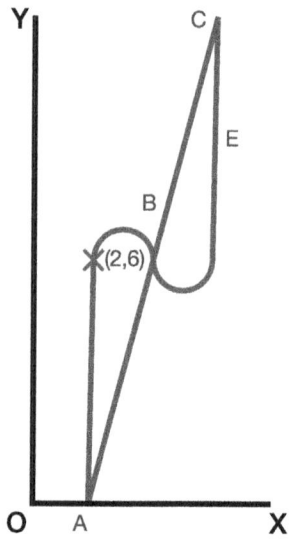

How Do You Know?

We now have curves. And the equation gets dramatically more complicated:

$$Y = x^3 - 9x^2 + 26x - 18$$

This demonstration made an impact on me when I read it. It shows so clearly how adding one simple data point totally wrecks the simplicity of the old equation. It serves as a little mental model to remind you that adding another factor to your analysis likely complicates things more than you realize. So I pass it along to you with the hope that it may have a similar impact.

Another demonstration of this that I found quite memorable comes from author William O'Hanlon. I first came across it in Gad Horowitz's *The Book of Radical General Semantics*.

You have probably heard the old phrase "connecting the dots." I know financial writers who will sometimes say they help their readers "connect the dots."

Well, you can understand O'Hanlon's graphic if you keep that old saw in mind. Now, imagine we have 18 dots. We've arranged them in six columns and four rows as shown here:

Let's Connect the Dots

```
•   •   •   •   •   •
•   •   •   •   •   •
•   •   •   •   •   •
•   •   •   •   •   •
```

Let the dots represent 'facts.' Now we want to "connect the dots," or make sense of them. O'Hanlon's chart shows some of the ways in which you can connect the dots.

It's a brilliant rendering and makes clear there are many ways to interpret the same set of facts.

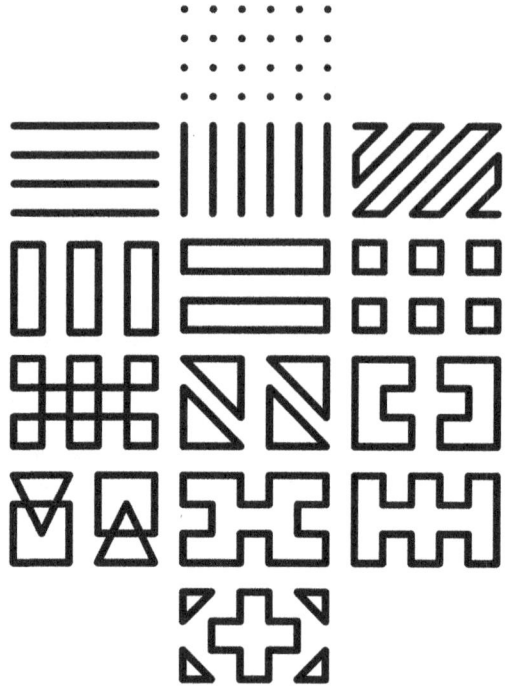

And as Horowitz notes:

> O'Hanlon's diagram presupposes that everyone agrees that the dots
> account for all relevant facts and they all are equally important.
> However, in the soft sciences, human relations, etc., these criteria are
> rarely if ever satisfied.

Indeed. In the real world, different people will use different dots, or more dots
(or fewer). It's endless. As O'Hanlon's chart makes clear, no one interpretation
is any better or worse than any other. They are all possible, plausible ways to
"connect the dots."

Examples of Cause and Effect Going Awry: Business Delusions

Phil Rosenzweig's *The Halo Effect... and the Eight Other Business Delusions
That Deceive Managers* shows you how you can go wrong following seemingly
plausible cause-and-effect analysis. In the process, he eviscerates a couple of
business blockbusters.

One of them is *In Search of Excellence: Lessons from America's Best-Run Companies* (1982) by Tom Peters and Bob Waterman. *In Search of Excellence* seemed well-researched, and the authors had a good pedigree as both were working for McKinsey & Co., a well-regarded consulting firm.

The book asked a simple question: Why are some companies more successful than others? The authors came up with a list of companies after a rigorous process and careful selection. These "best" companies included Boeing, Caterpillar, Delta Air Lines, IBM, Johnson & Johnson, McDonald's, 3M, and others.

Then they did lots of interviews and gathered data – and finally, they found what they thought made companies excellent. The list included such things as: a bias for action, staying close to the customer, autonomy and entrepreneurship, among other attributes (which, as an aside, are awful murky on the face of it).

But the problem is that no matter how much research they did, their quest was doomed from the start for reasons we've addressed in this section.

Rosenzweig, with the benefit of hindsight (*Halo Effect* came out in 2007), checked on how the *Excellent* companies performed after the book came out. "How well did they do?" Rosenzweig asked. "Not very well."

Between 1980 and 1984, the S&P 500 almost doubled. Meanwhile, of the 35 companies on which there was public data (some were private, or were divisions of larger companies), only 12 did better. The others lagged the market.

If you go out 10 years, the results are about the same. "You would have been better off investing in a market index than putting your money on those *Excellent* companies," Rosenzweig writes. "Most of the companies weren't even *average*, never mind *Excellent*."

Lest you think this is a one-off, Rosenzweig repeats the experiment with another business blockbuster, *Built to Last: Successful Habits of Visionary Companies* (1994) by Jim Collins and Jerry Porras. In this case, the authors started with 200 top companies and winnowed them down to "the best of the best." Again, you have a roll call of seemingly great businesses: IBM, Motorola, American Express, Merck, Disney, and more.

And these were great businesses: A dollar invested in the S&P 500 in 1926 grew to $415 by 1990. But a dollar invested in each of these *Visionary* firms would have grown to $6,356.

So, what was their secret? Collins and Porras created their own list of essentials:

- Having a strong core ideology that guides the company's decisions and behavior

- Building a strong corporate culture

- Setting audacious goals

- Developing people and promoting from within

- Creating a spirit of experimentation and risk-taking

- Driving for excellence

Sounds wonderful (and also murky to identify in the real world). But, again, the results were not so hot. In the five years after the book came out, only eight of the 17 publicly-traded companies outperformed the market. (One company was privately held and excluded from this test.) Rosenzweig concludes: "You would have been better off investing randomly than putting your money on Collins and Porras's *Visionary* companies." Ouch.

It wasn't just market performance. Business performance actually declined:

> For the five years after the study ended, only five companies improved their profitability while eleven declined, with one unchanged. Whether we look to market performance or profit performance, the picture is the same: Most of Collins and Porras's *Visionary* companies, chosen precisely because they had done so well for so long, fell back to earth.

Collins would try again with *Good to Great: Why Some Companies Make the Leap... and Others Don't* (2001). This time he really wanted to crack the code. He and his team spent five years and over 15,000 hours on the project. They read dozens of books and more than 6,000 articles and compiled data that totaled over 384 million bytes. Once again, Collins had a new list of companies and another best-seller... But do we really need to go over what happened to the *Great* companies?

In "Good to Great, or Just Good?" Bruce Niendorf and Kristine Beck (2008) conclude:

In terms of long-term stock return performance, the Good to Great firms do not differ significantly from the average company on the S&P 500. Our evidence is consistent with the conclusion that although the Good to Great firms may be good, they aren't great.

And two of 11, Fannie Mae and Circuit City, would turn out as essentially zeros barely six years later!

The above ought to create in you a great sense of humility. And it ought to lead you to distrust a great deal of what passes for cause-and-effect analysis these days. We don't really know what makes a company great. We don't really know most of the things we think we do. Therefore, to clarify your thinking, you must learn to distrust (and question) cause-and-effect analysis wherever you find it.

Key Takeaways

- Cause and effect are tricky to determine, perhaps impossible. You should learn to distrust such thinking that runs along the lines of "If X then Y."

- Remember David Leinweber's "Stupid Data Miner Tricks" linking Bangladesh butter production, its sheep population and U.S. cheese production as "predicting" the returns of the S&P 500. I've pulled his example out in many conversations, and it always makes the point well. You can find Leinweber's paper online.

- We introduced Alan Watts' cat and tail analogy here – another good analogy that shows how little we know about cause and effect.

- We saw how we can represent a line with a simple equation and how that equation gets way more complicated with the addition of just one point not on the line. A reminder of how complex our world is.

- We looked at O'Hanlon's "The Reality of Reality," a brilliant graphic that shows how many ways we can interpret the same set of 'facts.'

- Phil Rosenzweig's The Halo Effect... and the Eight Other Business Delusions That Deceive Managers shows you how you can go wrong following seemingly plausible cause-and-effect analysis.

Chapter 3

Don't Trust Labels

"You eat ideas and wear labels!"

~ U.G. Krishnamurti (1918-2007), philosopher, as quoted in *Goner: The Final Travels of U.G. Krishnamurti* by Louis Brawley

I love the work from the fertile minds of Murray Stahl and Steven Bregman at the money management firm Horizon Kinetics. They have a way of piercing Wall Street's abstractions and revealing an underlying reality quite different from what you'd expect.

In this chapter, we're going to look at why you can't trust labels.

In *Compendium Compilation: Selected Essays Published in 2016* by Murray Stahl, he often shows the dangers of relying on generalizations and labels. We covered this idea earlier, but it's worth pulling out and considering on its own.

Stahl looked at the VanEck Vectors Coal ETF (KOL). This is an ETF made up of a basket of coal companies. Presumably, people who buy this ETF want to get exposure to coal.

But as Stahl asks: "Should someone investing in this fund know something about the various companies in order to form a generalized premise about the fund?" My answer would be yes. I can't buy a bucket of stocks blind. I want to know what's in the bucket. ETF investors often don't bother to look.

If you look at what's in KOL, you find some interesting things, as Stahl shows.

The idea behind a coal ETF is that it gets you exposure to coal. You'd expect to find coal miners. Jastrzebska Spolka is one coal miner in the index. It mines coal in Poland, most of which stays in Poland.

"This is just one company," Stahl writes. "The fund has 28 holdings. Imagine meeting 28 people about which you know nothing except that they are all employed in the coal mining industry in one capacity or another. Now imagine being asked to make true generalizations about those people as a group."

I'd say that would be very difficult. And I'd also agree that such generalizations would not be worth much. Such is the case with KOL. The companies are all very different. You can see it in the performance of the stocks in the ETF.

The Polish stock was up 3.5x in 2016 through July 2016 when Stahl wrote his essay. But another stock in the coal ETF was the oddly named Korean coal firm Kiwi Media, which Stahl points out *fell* 45%.

Beyond performance, many of the stocks in KOL are in widely different businesses. One holding in the ETF was Joy Global, which doesn't even mine coal, but sells equipment to miners. FreightCar America was also in the coal ETF but doesn't mine coal either. It ships coal, among other commodities. The point is they are all very different. Is the logic underlying a coal ETF sound?

There are worse offenders...

My favorite might be the PowerShares Dynamic Leisure & Entertainment ETF (PEJ). The fund had $132 million in assets. Presumably all the people who put money here were looking to get exposure to the leisure and entertainment industry.

Once again, the obvious conclusion is wrong.

As Stahl pointed out, the top holdings of PEJ included some baffling choices. McDonald's was the third-largest holding at 5% of the fund. The next largest holdings – slots 4 through 8 – were as follows:

Southwest Airlines, 4.9%

American Airlines, 4.9%

United Continental Holdings, 4.7%

Delta Air Lines, 4.4%

SkyWest Airlines, 3.2%

All airlines.

That's about a quarter of the fund in airline stocks. Sounds like an airline ETF to me. As Stahl joked, "Perhaps the logic is one needs to fly before one can have entertainment, and while one is being entertained, what is better than a Big Mac?"

Even stranger, PEJ didn't own obvious choices, such as Disney. Nor did it own Lions Gate Entertainment, which makes movies. It even has "entertainment" in the name.

A funny duck that PEJ is...

Even when ETFs have a similar name, you can't trust that they'll be the same.

Todd Rosenbluth at ETF.com has a couple of choice examples in a piece called "ETFs That Sound Alike Are Often Different."

He compares two ETFs: the Vanguard Telecommunications Services ETF (VOX) and the SPDR S&P Telecom ETF (XTL). The former has 20%-plus weightings in AT&T and Verizon. It has smaller positions in CenturyLink, Level 3 Communications, and T-Mobile USA and no stocks from other sectors of the telecom universe.

The SPDR S&P Telecom ETF (XTL), on the other hand, has about 60% in communications equipment companies such as Arista Networks and Palo Alto Networks. And then it has equally weighted positions in the aforementioned telecom service providers.

These differences matter because it comes out in the performance. "XTL outperformed VOX by more than 200 basis points in 2016," Rosenbluth notes, "but underperformed by 400 basis points in 2015, a reminder that when the constituents are different, the records will also be." These are wide gaps in performance between two assets labeled "Telecom ETF."

He also looks at two homebuilding ETFs:

> Both the SPDR S&P Homebuilders ETF (XHB) and the iShares U.S. Home Construction ETF (ITB) have approximately $1.1 billion in assets and trade about 2 million shares on a daily basis. Yet despite XHB's name, the ETF has just 30% of assets in homebuilder stocks, less than half the percentage that can be found in ITB.

> While ITB has double-digit weightings in its two largest holdings, DR Horton and Lennar [both homebuilders], XHB's top positions include Whirlpool and Johnson Controls [not homebuilders].

I wonder how many people pay attention to those differences. I'm guessing not many at all...

Investing blindly, or by labels only, is the way investing is going today – more and more money flowing into more and more ETFs. It's industrial investing, like industrial farming. It doesn't have to taste like a real tomato. It just has to look like one so they can sell it to you.

But not anymore, because armed with the ideas in this book, you'll know what questions to ask and what you're getting into.

The Power of a Name

"As a rule, when people realize they do not understand a thing they try *to find a name* for what they do not 'understand,' and when they find a name they say they 'understand.' But to 'find a name' does not mean to 'understand.' Unfortunately, people are usually satisfied with names."

~ G.I. Gurdjieff as quoted in P.D. Ouspensky's *In Search of the Miraculous*

I've always been fascinated by how you can give something a name and that name can completely change the way people view that thing.

This is an old trick, well known by advertisers. In "Would Carrots by Any Other Name Taste as Sweet?" Nicholas Bakalar of *The New York Times* reported on a study that showed how "college students would rather eat 'slow-roasted caramelized zucchini bites' than just plain 'zucchini,' even when both dishes are prepared exactly the same way."

This was a study that involved 27,933 customers over 46 days in a college cafeteria, of whom 8,279 selected vegetables. The *Times*:

> Each day, the experimenters varied the names of the dishes to create a different gustatory impression. The basic "carrots" served one day became the healthful but somewhat stern "carrots with sugar-free citrus dressing" the next, then mutated into the still health-conscious but more friendly "smart-choice vitamin C citrus carrots," and finally achieved metamorphosis as the restaurant-menu worthy "twisted citrus-glazed carrots."

> Giving a vegetable dish a creative name – like "zesty ginger-turmeric sweet potatoes" instead of just plain "sweet potatoes" – resulted in 25% more people choosing the vegetable. But 35% more customers chose the zesty label than the health-positive "wholesome sweet potato superfood," and 41 percent more chose it than the scolding "cholesterol-free sweet potatoes."

I read this and smiled. It's what I'd expect to see. And the principle works in the markets, too. When the internet was hot back in the 1990s tech boom, some companies would change their name to add "dot com." And their stocks would pop.

What's funny is that after the tech crash, companies would change their name again. This time they'd drop "dot com," and their stocks would soar. And it didn't just happen in the 1990s. In the 1960s, the same thing happened with "electronics" when it was the hot thing. There are papers written about this phenomenon of name changes driving significant changes in stock prices.

Anyway, an anecdote from the tech bubble will tell you all you need to know.

In 1999, there was a company called The Publishing Co. of North America Inc. Enviously eyeing the booming market for internet shares, management decided to change the company's name to Attorneys.com. The stock doubled.

Then the tech bubble burst. The stock fell more than 75% from its 2000 peak. Well, the firm decided to change its name again. This time it took on 1-800-Attorney. In days, the stock jumped 40%. (See "For Dot-Coms, New Names Can Give Pop to a Stock" by Ken Brown in *The Wall Street Journal*).

And the professors want to tell us the market is "efficient." Uh-huh.

Still, I see this naming trick at work all the time. The ETF examples above fit. Think about it: All PowerShares had to do to get $132 million in assets was to put together a fund and call it "leisure and entertainment." They can put whatever they want in it apparently and investors don't seem to care. PowerShares executives are probably chuckling over it right now and wondering what else they can get away with.

But here's another interesting comparison from C.T. Fitzpatrick in his 2016 third-quarter letter to shareholders. Fitzpatrick is the chief investment officer at Vulcan Value Partners, an investment advisory based in Birmingham, Alabama.

Consider Post Properties, an Atlanta-based apartment REIT. REIT stands for real estate investment trust. It's a popular way to own real estate. It's also a popular type of stock to own right now because REITs (by rule) pay out most of their earnings in dividends.

So, Mid-America acquired Post at a price of 26x free cash flow. This valuation was not out of line with most REITs, but Post is arguably a worse asset than most REITs.

Fitzpatrick writes: "While higher quality retail and office REITs have longer leases ranging from 3 to 10 years, apartment REITs generally turn over roughly half of their units annually. So just to break even, they have to resell half of their product annually before they can grow."

Now, consider Oracle. People don't call Oracle a "REIT." Yet, it has long-term contracts (licensing agreements). These even have inflation-adjusted escalators, just like a lease. Oracle enjoys over 90% customer retention. And it can add customers without having to build a new apartment.

"In real estate terms," Fitzpatrick tells us, "Oracle can grow its 'occupancy' without physical constraints. ... Moreover, unlike REITs, which are highly leveraged, Oracle has net cash on its balance sheet. So Oracle can grow twice as fast as the typical REIT without leverage. Adjusted for cash, Oracle trades at less than 11.5 times free cash flow."

So, let's see... Oracle has a business that in its essential characteristics is much like a real estate firm. Except, it is better. It has cash, no net debt. It's growing faster. And yet the market values it at half what the acquirer paid for Post.

Strange. It's almost as if the market says, "Well, Post is a REIT." And you say, "Yes, but clearly Oracle is a far superior asset in every respect." And the market comes back and says, "Yes, but... Post is a REIT." (Shades of *Spinal Tap*'s "these go to eleven.")

Hedge funds also benefit from the word magic of names. A new study, "Hedge Fund Flows and Name Gravitas," by professors Juha Joenväärä and Cristian Ioan Tiu shows how investors favor hedge funds with names that "exhibit gravitas – defined as a combination of words from geopolitics and economics, or suggesting power."

It seems absurd, but the professors find that "adding one more word with gravitas to the name of the average fund brings more than a quarter million dollars more in annual flows."

The power of names! Don't trust them.

Key Takeaways

- You should distrust labels. All labels, like all maps, are abstractions and do not represent the thing they name. Labels leave things out. These details can be important.

- To show this, we looked at several ETFs and how they're labeled. One example: an entertainment and leisure ETF with a quarter of its assets in airlines – and yet no position in Disney. Another was a homebuilder ETF with less than 30% of its assets in homebuilders.

- We also looked at how differences in the companies in any ETF undermine the idea that they all represent a play on a theme.

- We looked at the power of a name and how it can drive stock prices in the short term. During the dot-com boom of the 1990s, companies would add "dot com" to their name, and their stocks would soar.

- Remember, just because you know what other people call a thing doesn't mean you understand anything about it. Look past names and labels, and try to get at the underlying reality.

Chapter 4

We Can't See the World Objectively

"'I only decide about my Universe,' continued the man [who is the ruler of the universe] quietly. 'My Universe is my eyes and my ears. Anything else is hearsay.'

'But you don't believe in anything?' [Zarniwoop asks].

The man shrugged and picked up his cat.

'I don't understand what you mean,' he said.

'You don't understand that what you decide in this shack of yours affects the lives and fates of millions of people? This is all monstrously wrong!'

'I don't know. I've never met all these people you speak of. And neither, I suspect, have you. They only exist in words we hear. It is folly to say you know what is happening to other people. Only they know, if they exist. They have their own Universes of their eyes and ears.'"

~ Douglas Adams (1952-2001), *The Restaurant at the End of the Universe*

"Each being is, exactly as you are, the sole centre of a Universe in no wise identical with, or even assimilable to, your own. The impersonal Universe of "Nature" is only an abstraction, approximately true, of the factors which it is convenient to regard as common to all. The Universe of another is therefore necessarily unknown to, and unknowable by, you."

~ Aleister Crowley (1875-1947)

So far, we've talked about how we abstract from the world around us. And we've seen why we should distrust those abstractions and the inferences we draw from them (such as with labels and cause-and-effect analysis).

In this chapter, we look at another limitation: our own point of view. As R.D. Carmichael, a physicist, said: "The universe, as known to us, is a joint phenomenon of the observer and the observed."

In other words, you can't take the observer out of the analysis. Whatever we observe, we observe through the filter of our own nervous system. We cannot forget this important point.

Ice is cold, but it requires a point of view to register the cold, a human being via a nervous system or through an instrument such as a thermometer.

More than just providing a point of view, our nervous system plays an active role in what we see. We don't just sit and watch – we "create," to some degree, what we see. Our experiences, our beliefs, our particular vantage point... among other things... all impact what we think we see.

A fun way to appreciate this is through the work of Adelbert Ames Jr. (1880-1955). Ames is most famous as the creator of a variety of "demonstrations" of impossible things, of illusions. I recently read a biography on Ames by W.C. Bamberger, *A Life of Vision and Becomingness*. The back cover includes a summary of some of these demonstrations:

> Rooms where small children tower over their parents, where water runs uphill; he created demonstrations where playing cards and cigarette packs and matchbooks seem to change size and position in the blink of an eye, where stationary balloons seem to draw near then move away, where chairs deconstruct into wires and white trapezoids, and where a steel bar bends around a rotating window frame.

One of his famous demonstrations – the Ames room – is nearby.

The Ames Room – A Trick of Perspective

The trick is one of perspective. The smaller figure on the left is simply further back. The windows are not the same size either. The one on the left is actually bigger than the one on the right. And the room shrinks as it moves from left to right. You can see how it's done in the second picture nearby, "How the Ames Room Works."

How the Ames Room Works

But it's impossible to see this, even when you know how it's done!

Ames used his many demonstrations to develop theories of perception. The idea that we "see" objectively crumbles under his analysis. Instead, you come to understand that the brain makes "gambles." The brain makes what it "sees" fit with what it knows or has already seen. If the eye was not an objective instrument, Ames thought, then perhaps all knowledge was equally subjective and unreliable.

Uncomfortable ideas. And in Ames' time they were cutting edge. But now they've become largely accepted. I read about Ames and couldn't stop thinking about how his work applied to markets. It makes one – again, there is no other word – humble. It's possible what we think we see is simply a trick of perspective. Perhaps our minds craft a story... and that story is not real.

One of my favorite demonstrations of this – not from Ames – is what I call "The Square That Isn't There." (See nearby graphic.)

The Square That Isn't There

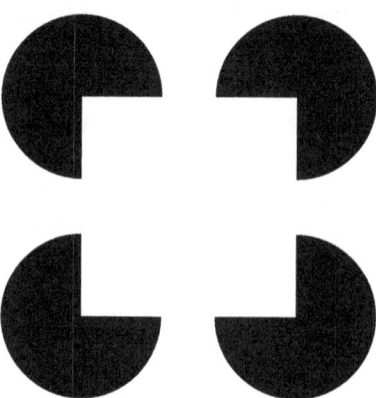

If you're normal, you "see" a white square. But look carefully, and you'll see how your 'mind' is squaring off the image for you. There are no lines forming a square in that picture. It's very hard to look at this image and not see a square, even when you know it isn't there.

Both Ames' demonstrations and the square that isn't there show how we've got some 'hard-wiring.' We have limits to our perception that we can't get around. Some of these limits are obvious. We can't see infrared light or microwaves, or radio signals. We can't hear beyond a certain band on the spectrum either. Some of the limits are less obvious, such as the tricks of perception Ames reveals. Knowing that these limitations exist ought to create a sense of humility about what you think you 'see.'

One final example: an experiment that I first read about in one of Robert Anton Wilson's books (more on him below), but which comes originally from Korzybski. It's a simple experiment that you can try out at home with someone.

You select newspaper headlines, all about the same size. Then you have your subject sit in a chair. You pull back to some distance and ask if he or she can read the headline. If they can, you take the next headline and move back a little further. You keep going until you find you are just outside of the range of legibility.

Now, when you've reached this spot where your subject cannot read the headline, you read the headline to your subject. An interesting thing happens. Whereas before they could not read the headline, now they can. They will usually 'see' the headline when they know what they are supposed see.

How Do You Know?

As Korzybski writes:

> The question arises, what part in the 'seeing' is due to 'senses,' and what to 'mind'? The answer is, that, structurally, the 'seeing' is the result of a cyclic *interdependent* process, which can be *split only verbally*.

In other words, 'seeing' is something the whole organism does. The entire human nervous system as an entity 'sees.'

We're going to pause here and linger over a point Korzybski makes in that quote. He says, "which can be *split only verbally*." What does he mean?

Keep It Together: Elementalistic Thinking vs. Non-Elementalistic Thinking

Korzybski saw the act of splitting verbally what wasn't split in the nonverbal world as a neurolinguistic flaw. He called it elementalistic thinking. This stands in contrast to non-elementalistic thinking (or el versus non-el). El thinking means you split things verbally that are not split in the non-verbal world.

The *Oxford English Dictionary* (second edition) credits Korzybski with coining this usage of elementalism:

> The verbal separation into separate concepts or entities of things which cannot be separated empirically or physically, e.g., space and time, body and mind.

'Mind' and 'body' is a classic example of el thinking. These exist separately only verbally. In the non-verbal world we inhabit, there are no 'minds' without 'bodies.' The same is true of 'space' and 'time.' We could add to this list the words 'observer' and 'observed,' concepts we can separate verbally but that in the non-verbal world are always together. There is no observer or observed without the other. 'Thoughts' and 'feelings' is another common bit of el thinking. Semanticists like to say thinking-feeling.

Non-el thinking, then, aims to keep it all together. The cure, as Robert Pula wrote in his *Glossary*, is to use a hyphen. Therefore, "not space *and* time, but space-time; not mind *and* body, but mind-body; not observer *and* observed, but observer-observed." (We'll talk more about the hyphen in Part II.)

If it seems strange to go around talking and writing in this hyphenated way, I would agree. It can be useful to use those terms, sans hyphen, as a matter of expediency or in casual talk. But keep in mind the distinction between el and non-el when you want to engage in a more careful evaluation.

Remember, a key aim of general semantics is to make our maps (ideas, etc.) match up better with the facts. To do that, we should be mindful not to split things verbally that are not split in the real world.

Investors commonly praise the performance of a CEO by looking at what the stock did under his watch. This is likely misplaced cause and effect at work. But you could also argue that you cannot separate the CEO from his company in this way.

El thinking often comes about when we try to find the cause of something. As Martin Levinson, a general semanticist author, writes:

> Elementalism is involved when we seek *the* cause of something, unconsciously assuming that there is only one cause. For example, *the* cause of juvenile delinquency, *the* cure for cancer, *the* way to raise children, etc. But most problems in life do not have single antecedents. Causation is typically multi-faceted.

Non-el thinking tries to keep together what is together in the non-verbal world, even though our language so easily separates them.

So we know now we must consider the observer and the observed. But we shouldn't stop there either. We have to consider the observer and the observed and the environment. Or, as general semanticists like to say, "the organism as a whole in an environment." That's the basic unit of analysis. And the reason is that the environment also impacts the observer and the observed.

The point of general semantics, as I see it, is to 'clean up' our neurolinguistic processes, to make the world inside our skulls more in tune with the world outside of our skulls.

The point Korzybski and his merry band make again and again is that the world outside of our skulls has a structure. And Korzybski's idea was to make our way of talking and thinking about it match up better with that structure. As he wrote:

All that we deal with in the outside world involves indivisibly 'matter,' 'space,' and 'time.' Using the old language, there cannot be something somewhere at 'no time,' or something at some 'time' and 'no where' or 'nothing' 'somewhere' at 'some time.' **Everything which happens must be structurally represented as something, somewhere, at some 'time.'** If the structure of the world happened to be such that 'nothing' would happen 'nowhere' at 'no time,' then we would have nothing to talk about, and all we would or could say would deal with our fancies. [Bold added.]

The Guerilla Ontologist: We Make Our World

To get back to our main thread: We are not passive viewers on the scene. We see actively. We make our world, in many respects; we see what we want to see. You must always consider the observer(s).

Robert Anton Wilson (or RAW as his fans call him) is probably most famous as the author of *The Illuminatus! Trilogy*, a fictional satirical romp laced with conspiracy, sex, and occult references. To me, however, his best books are a different trilogy entirely: *Cosmic Trigger I*, *Prometheus Rising*, and *Quantum Psychology*.

These are nonfiction books and not meant as any kind of trilogy, it's just how I think of them. Each book is a mind-bending exploration of oddball ideas. They are a lot of fun to read, as long as you don't take anything too seriously. (In fact, this is worthy advice for life generally.)

RAW was a playful thinker, a self-described "guerilla ontologist." He enjoyed pushing the boundaries of what you think likely or possible. He wrote about contact with UFOs and premonition, but he also wrote about quantum physics and transactional psychology. He ranges over a whole series of fringy thinkers such as Crowley, Timothy Leary, John Lilly, and many more. You are never sure what he really believes. He cultivates this doubt and practically begs his readers early on in *Cosmic Trigger* to understand that he is truly agnostic – about everything.

"The agnostic attitude is revealed again and again in the text," he writes in the preface to *Cosmic Trigger*, "but many people still think I 'believe' some of the metaphors and models employed here. I therefore want to make it even clearer than ever before that **I DO NOT BELIEVE ANYTHING**."

Or, in another formulation of the same idea in *Email to the Universe*, RAW adds a caveat: "I don't believe anything, but I have many suspicions." This has become my motto.

He called his philosophy "maybe logic," and the idea was to embrace the uncertainty of life. As he wrote in *Email to the Universe*, "If my books do what I intend, they should leave the reader feeling that the universe is capable of doing something totally shocking and unexpected in the next five minutes. I am trying to show that life without certainty can be exhilarating, liberating, a great adventure."

In that I'd say he succeeded. RAW was also an admirer of Alfred Korzybski. In a speech at the Harvard Club in 1997, RAW gave a "rough rundown on how Korzybski continues to influence me." (The title of his talk was "The Map Is Not the Territory: The Future Is Not the Past," a wonderful address that you can find online.)

He said:

> All the events that are going on in the world I tend to see through a Korzybskian grid. He made a bigger impression on me than just about any writer I have ever read.

That Korzybskian grid is evident in all his books and is one of the reasons I like them. He wrote from a non-Aristotelian perspective, pointing out the folly of our abstractions and the limitations of our knowledge.

The Thinker and the Prover

In *Prometheus Rising*, RAW begins by exploring an idea he borrows from Dr. Leonard Orr – the idea that our brains function as if they had two halves, a "thinker" and a "prover." (These are abstractions, I probably need not remind you, but instructive in their way.)

The "thinker" can think of almost anything – that the dollar is going to seed, that a recession is around the corner, that the market will crash... or that the market will rally, that the economy will boom, that stocks are cheap...

The "prover" then seeks to prove whatever the "thinker" thinks:

> If the Thinker thinks that the sun moves around the earth, the Prover will obligingly organize all perceptions to fit that thought; if the Thinker changes its mind and decides the earth moves around the sun, the Prover will reorganize the evidence.

This theory holds remarkably well, even among highly intelligent people. RAW gives the example of Einstein, who resisted quantum theory despite repeated experiments that supported it. And Edison committed himself to direct current (DC) electrical generators and insisted alternating current (AC) generators were unsafe.

As RAW points out, these scientists – and there are many more examples – as brilliant as they were, were still human beings subject to the same limitations we've talked about here.

"Science achieves, or approximates, objectivity not because the individual scientist is immune from the psychological laws that govern the rest of us," RAW wrote, "but because scientific method... eventually overrides individual prejudices, in the long run."

In the short run, it's Orr's law: "Whatever the Thinker thinks, the Prover will prove." This idea is widely accepted today and usually goes by the more formal name of confirmation bias, though I prefer the more colorful Orr's law. Whatever you want to call it, it is something we have to guard against if we're going to be successful in markets.

The way out is to adopt what RAW calls "model agnosticism." However we organize our thoughts, these thoughts hang together in what we can consider a kind of model of the world "out there." RAW's "model agnosticism" then means that you do not commit to any one model. "'Reality' is always plural and mutable," as he says in *Cosmic Trigger*. (Spend some time with RAW's books and you'll see Korzybski's influence all over.)

To use another favorite phrase of RAW's coined by his friend Timothy Leary, we all have our "reality tunnels." We can never really get completely out of our own reality tunnels. Although many have tried. (Some popular ways to do this include the use of psychedelics and other drugs and/or various mystical practices and rituals, etc., to "alter consciousness" and perceptions.)

We can still cultivate in ourselves a certain detachment, a willingness to concede that our view is just one view – and not to cling to it.

Psychology of Intelligence Analysis

In 1999, the Center for the Study of Intelligence published a book by Richards J. Heuer Jr. called *Psychology of Intelligence Analysis*. (You can find the book for free on the CIA's website. Just Google the title and it comes right up.) The Center is an organization within the CIA. And Heuer worked for the CIA for 45 years. The book collects articles Heuer wrote during 1978-86 for use within the CIA.

He based his work on a review of cognitive psychology literature that deals with how people process information and make judgments on incomplete and ambiguous information. As I probably don't need to tell you, this is exactly what investors have to do.

Heuer's book fits perfectly with what we're talking about here, as a choice quote illustrates:

> A central focus of this book is to illuminate the role of the observer in determining what is observed and how it is interpreted. **People construct their own version of "reality" on the basis of information provided by the senses,** but this sensory input is mediated by complex mental processes that determine which information is attended to, how it is organized, and the meaning attributed to it. What people perceive, how readily they perceive it, and how they process this information after receiving it are all strongly influenced by past experience, education, cultural values, role requirements, and organizational norms, as well as by the specifics of the information received. [Bold added.]

In a slight twist to what we've talked about so far, Heuer shows how we tend to see what we *expect* to see. And he maintains this is a more important tendency than seeing what we *want* to see. There are many experiments that show this. One simple one is nearby. (See "You see what you expect to see.")

You see what you expect to see

Source: *Psychology of Intelligence Analysis,* p. 8

The vast majority of people, when they see those three triangles, will miss something about them. (Look again. The article is written twice in each of the three phrases.) Our brains automatically and effortlessly seem to make what we see conform to what we expect.

That's interesting, but it has an important corollary principle: "It takes more information, and more unambiguous information, to recognize an unexpected phenomenon than an expected one."

This is no surprise to those of us who have spent time in markets and have held stocks under a certain belief we were slow to change in the face of mounting evidence our view was wrong. It usually takes something of a "shock" to snap us out of our expectation-based reality tunnel. Of course, by then it is often too late.

This is really hard to get around, because we need to have some 'mind-set' around which we organize the flood of sensory inputs we receive. As Heuer says, 'mind-sets' are slow to change; gradual, evolutionary change often passes unnoticed.

Heuer cites experiments that show how prolonged exposure to blurred images makes it more difficult for us to recognize the image even as it gradually sharpens, than someone who comes along at a later stage – with less time exposed to the blurred image. The latter were able recognize the image in less time. Put another way, the longer people were exposed to a blurred image, the clearer the picture had to become before they recognized it. (Evidence for the value of that old saw about having "a fresh set of eyes" look at this problem...)

Another important idea in Heuer's book that I want to include here stands against the prevailing wisdom that more information improves our decision-making. This is a particular vice of investors, some of whom can put together incredibly impressive and lengthy slide presentations. The detail and research are amazing, but then you have to wonder where the point of diminishing returns is.

Heuer cites experiments that show experienced analysts (from a variety of fields) need a certain minimum amount of information to make an informed judgment, after which his or her accuracy does not improve with additional information.

A memorable example from horse racing shows how handicappers' accuracy did not improve when they were given more than a handful of key variables. But their confidence rose, as the nearby chart shows.

More Information makes us more confident, but not more accurate

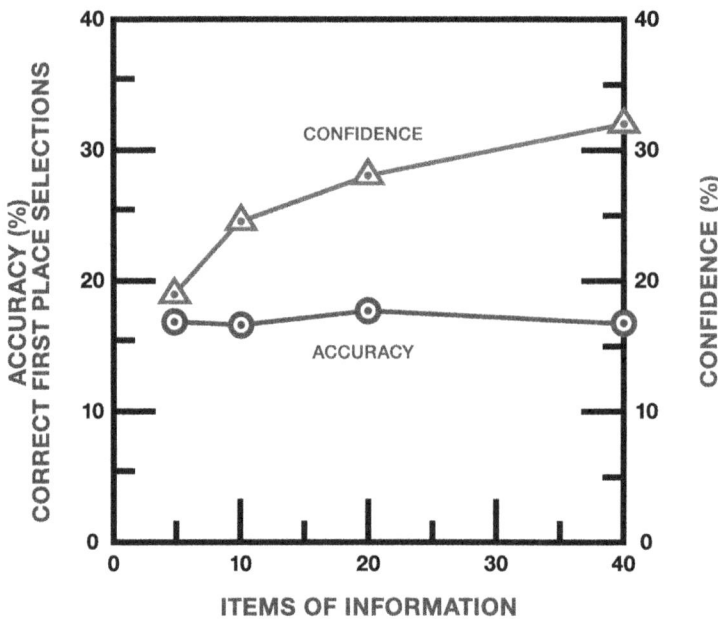

Source: *Psychology of Intelligence Analysis*, p. 54

Our mental models are simpler than we think, needing a smaller number of essential variables to make an informed judgment. Beyond that, we're just making ourselves feel better (more confident).

I think Heuer would've liked Korzybski's work, if he didn't already know about it. Suffice to say, Heuer's book is worth a read, especially if you've not had much exposure to behavioral finance. (For more on behavioral psychology and its specific applications to investing, see James Montier's massive *Behavioural Investing: A Practitioner's Guide to Applying Behavioral Finance*.)

In summary, we labor under some enormous handicaps in our effort to perceive the world around us and behave rationally. There is a steady stream of books from cognitive scientists, it seems, and the conclusions are not encouraging. (See for example "That's What You Think" by Elizabeth Kolbert, *The New Yorker*, February 27, 2017.)

But don't despair. Instead, think how lucky it is that nobody knows anything. It levels the playing field, in a way. Adopting the type of thinking and tools I suggest will go a long way towards giving you a leg up on people who seem much smarter than you are. We'll get to those tools and devices in Part II, but we have more ground to cover first...

Key Takeaways

- 'Reality' is a product of both the observer and the observed. We're not just passive observers; we create, to some extent, what we see.

- The experiments of Adelbert Ames Jr. show how our minds make "gambles" to fit what they see with what they expect. Ames' work leads us to question the idea of "objective" knowledge.

- Further, we can't stop with observer and observed. We have to consider the environment at hand.

- Robert Anton Wilson and his "guerilla ontology" reminds us to be skeptical of models of any kind.

- We have a Thinker and a Prover. What the Thinker thinks, the Prover proves. Call it a more colorful analogy for confirmation bias.

- We looked at Richards J. Heuer Jr.'s *Psychology of Intelligence Analysis*. It provides more evidence that we create our own reality.

- Heuer also shows how more information does not improve our decision-making.

Chapter 5

Value Is a Mirror of Itself

"In this view the differences of the world are not isolated objects encountering one another in conflict, but expressions of polarity. Opposites and differences have something between them, like the two faces of a coin; they do not meet as total strangers."

~ Alan Watts, *Psychotherapy East and West*

In Nicaragua for the Fifth Annual Bonner Family Wealth Forum at Rancho Santana, I gave a talk in which I shared something that probably surprised the audience. I revealed one of the biggest abstractions in all of investing...

I began by telling them that I've been studying businesses and how to value them for 25 years. What I try to find out is what the "intrinsic value" of a business is. What's it really worth?

And here's the surprising thing I've learned: There is no such thing as intrinsic value. It's an abstraction. It's made up. It doesn't exist as an independent, objective thing.

Value is entirely relative.

If I had a glass of water and an ounce of gold on a table and said you could take whatever you thought was worth more, you'd take the gold.

However, if I change the setting – say you'd been in a desert for two days without water and knew you'd not get any water for another couple of days – then the calculus is different, isn't it?

As I say, it's all relative...

And it's not just true in markets. This is how we understand the world around us. Up needs down. Light needs darkness. (As the philosopher Alan Watts put it, "Light shines in darkness because what else could it shine in?") Black needs white. Hello needs goodbye. Life needs death. Good needs evil. (Lao Tzu said, "When everyone recognizes goodness as good, there is already evil.") Inside needs outside. Tops don't exist without bottoms. And so and so on...

It's the same in markets. Contrasts and comparisons make the game. Context is everything.

A price-earnings ratio of 7 for the S&P 500 sounds cheap. (Even though I question whether the price-earnings ratio of 500 stocks means anything at all, let's overlook that for the moment.) A price-earnings ratio of 7 translates into an earnings yield of 14%. (Earnings yield is the inverse of P/E.) In 1982, The S&P 500 carried this valuation. As I write, the S&P 500 trades for about 25 times earnings, for an earnings yield of just under 4%. So, 14% sounds great from today's perspective.

But let's step back to 1982. You could buy a government bond and get 15% for 10 years. Now that 14% earnings yield doesn't sound quite as attractive. Take the 15% guaranteed on the government bond? Or take an uncertain 14% earnings yield from stocks? The decision is not so easy. Context makes the difference.

Even a stock with a price-earnings ratio of 2 is not necessarily a bargain. If it's a fraud, the stock could be worthless. A price-earnings ratio of 100 might be a bargain if earnings grow 1,000%.

Context, context, context...

Value is also about perception.

I heard a funny story from Rory Sutherland – the self-described "ad man" who writes the Wiki Man column at *The Spectator* – that shows this point about how perception changes the way we value something.

The story goes like this...

There is a train that goes from London to Paris. The question put to a bunch of engineers was, "How do we make the journey to Paris better?"

And they came up with a good engineering solution, which was to knock off about 40 minutes from the then-3.5-hour journey at a cost of about £6 billion. That's an unimaginative, but common, way to look at the problem. "Let's make the trip more efficient," the thinking goes. "That's creating 'value' for our customer."

But Sutherland had another idea. What you should do is pay top male and female supermodels to walk the length of the train, handing out free Château Pétrus for the entire duration of the journey. You'll have saved about £4 billion. And people will ask for the trains to be slowed down.

'Value' has many facets. True, there is value in making the trains go faster because for most people there is value in getting where they want to go in less time; but it's not the <u>only</u> value that comes from riding the train.

(He also tells another funny story involving Mustafa Kemal Atatürk, the founder and first leader of the Republic of Turkey. Atatürk wanted to secularize Turkey and wanted to discourage women from wearing a veil. Normal, boring leaders would have just simply banned the veil. But Atatürk was a lateral thinker. He made it compulsory for prostitutes to wear the veil. Suddenly you didn't see many veils...)

There is a real-life example of a company doing something close to what Sutherland suggests.

In 1973, Southwest struggled to fill planes on its Houston-to-Dallas route. So the co-founder, Herb Kelleher, and Lamar Muse (then CEO) hatched a plan to drop prices in half – to $13 a flight. It worked, and Southwest started to fill its planes.

However, Braniff International Airways, the largest airline operator in Texas, didn't just sit there and let Southwest take away passengers. Braniff also dropped its price to $13. In their excellent *Intelligent Fanatics Project*, authors Ian Cassel and Sean Iddings pick up the tale:

> This was a tremendous blow to Southwest. At the time, this route was relatively small for Braniff and the cheaper fare could have been sustained by its other operations. Southwest, on the other hand, could easily have gone bankrupt.

What to do, what to do... Southwest came up with a creative solution, Sutherland-style.

It offered fliers a choice: Pay $13 or pay the regular fare of $26 and get a complimentary fifth of Chivas Regal scotch, Crown Royal Canadian whisky, or Smirnoff vodka.

And guess what? Southwest attracted a lot of business travelers who put the cost of the flight on their expense report and took the booze. In fact, about 76% of fliers chose to pay $26. For a time, Southwest was one of the largest liquor distributors in Texas.

How Do You Know?

Again, value has many facets, and what you see is a mirror of what you're looking for. That's why I called my presentation "Value is a mirror of itself." It was a twist on Thomas Schelling's observation that the universe is a mirror of itself. Meaning, broadly speaking, that what we see reflects what we know, what we expect to see, etc.

Clear thinking demands you do not accept the notion of a mystical, objective 'intrinsic value.' Instead, you understand that all notions of value have meaning only in comparison to something else.

It's not only that value is relative, but that value is also inseparable from its environment. Price-earnings ratios do not exist in isolation, for example. They exist in an environment, one we must be sure never to forget.

Profits need losses. Cheap stocks only exist in contrast to expensive stocks. High pay exists only in a world with low pay. The concept of winners makes sense only when there are also losers. Demand needs supply. Every buyer must have a seller. I'm sure you can come up with your own examples.

The clear thinker accepts and appreciates – and sees – this unity and interdependence.

Key Takeaways

- There is no such thing as "intrinsic value." All value is relative and depends on context.

- Value depends on perception and has meaning only because we can compare.

- Remember the story Rory Sutherland told about speeding up the train versus having supermodels on board handing out free wine. And how Southwest Airlines became the largest liquor distributor in Texas for a time. Both show how value goes beyond simple numbers.

Chapter 6

Logical Fate

"If he contend, as sometimes he will contend, that he has defined all his terms and proved all his propositions, then either he is a performer of logical miracles or he is an ass; and, as you know, logical miracles are impossible."

~ Cassius Keyser (1862-1947), mathematician

Cassius Keyser (1862-1947) was a mathematician with a philosophical bent. He became a dear friend and important mentor of sorts for Korzybski. Keyser also developed an idea that Korzybski made part of his system: the idea of logical fate, or logical destiny. Or, less romantically, as Pula would say, "neurological inevitability."

Logical fate means from certain premises certain conclusions follow inevitably. Logical fate described the deterministic relationship between premise and conclusion. Thus, if you start out with false assumptions, logical destiny says you're fated to reach false conclusions – unless you accept an inconsistency. The near diagram shows how this works. (See "It is your destiny!")

It is your destiny!

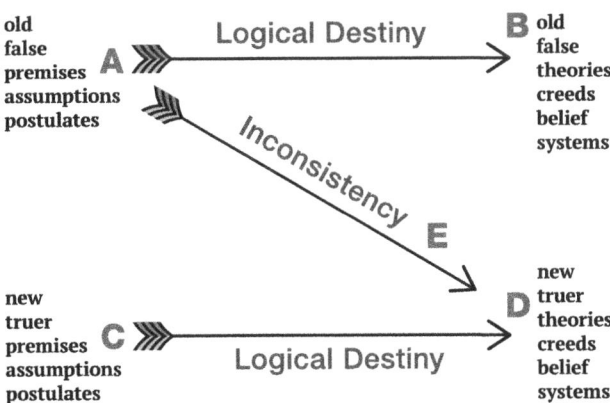

Let's look at a simple example to show how this works. The usual way in which we think tends to fall along syllogistic lines. The classic syllogism is:

All men are mortal

Socrates is a man

Socrates is mortal

But there is something interesting about this argument. Think about why it makes sense to you. Where does the logic derive? Does it come from the words, or from something else?

The answer: The structure of the argument is what gives it coherence. The words you can change. They are dispensable to the logic of the argument. And so you can reach a completely logical conclusion from utter nonsense.

See what happens when we change the words:

All gritches are a hogwashes

Michael is a gritch

Therefore, Michael is a hogwash

As Pula points out, "you can reach a correct, formally logical conclusion about nonsense. Schizophrenics do it often. Lewis Carroll did it for fun." In markets, I see this a lot.

GDP: A Bit of Nonsense

People will use GDP, for example, and they'll deduce something from that. But the question is never asked: What if the concept of GDP is itself nonsense? What if GDP is much like the gritch in the above syllogism?

It is a funny thing, GDP. Author Bill Bonner, a longtime colleague and friend, likes to tell a story about this: Two neighbors each cut their own grass. There is no addition to GDP. But if each cuts the other's grass for $20, then GDP goes up $40. Of course, nothing's changed. The 'economy' is not better off because they paid each other. What's changed is how we think about it.

The absurdities mount the more you play with it. If you get in a car accident, GDP goes up because you have to spend money fixing the car. If you get sick, GDP goes up because you have to spend money to get well. Basically, healthy people that don't get in accidents don't do anything for GDP, while sick people who get in accidents do. But I think we can all agree what world we'd rather live in.

Rory Sutherland points out that GDP is particularly bad at missing the value of the digital world. Wikipedia, for example, is like putting a free library in every home with internet access. Or think about any of the free content generated online by dozens of writers that otherwise you might never have heard from. "Does this massive new wealth register on GDP figures?" he asks. "Not a blip." Again, no money changes hands, so there is no impact on GDP.

Never mind all of the intangible things people value that GDP misses, such as leisure time. As Sutherland says, Europe could add 4% to its annual GDP if it adopted the U.S. standard of two weeks of vacation time. "Yet," he asks, "is there anyone in Europe who would willingly make this trade?"

In markets, we see people talk about earnings for the market, but, again, what if earnings are nonsense? Again, what if the concept is like a gritch, just something made up? It doesn't seem like that could be true, but look at the historical record, and you have to wonder. The earnings of many financial companies in 2006 and 2007 were not 'real.' The market gave them all back in 2008. They were built on the sand of a mortgage bubble.

And the quality of any number varies. Earnings in 2010 for a financial stock were different than in 2007. I would contend earnings of the later vintage were a higher quality, because they had been put through the ringer of the 2008 crisis.

I think we get into trouble because we don't realize that many of our classifications and words that we use are arbitrary and made-up. They don't refer to a physical reality.

The Paradox of the Barber

Let me tell show you this using the paradox of the barber, as told by general semanticist Harry L. Weinberg in his excellent *Levels of Knowing and Existence: Studies in General Semantics* (1959):

> In a certain town, there is a barber who shaves every man who does not shave himself. Does the barber shave himself?

How do you solve it?

There are many paradoxes like it. They all use the same trick. The paradox usually includes a word that you focus on and get stuck on. The word becomes a mental block blinding you to the obvious.

In this case, the word is "barber." Weinberg explains:

The paradox is unsolvable as long as one assumes that a man *is* a barber and this can be his only classification. The paradox dissolves when we realize that a man is classified as a barber only when he is barbering other people and that as soon as he barbers himself he is no longer a barber but is now to be classified as a man who shaves himself.

If we leave out the category "barber" and just say, "There is a man in town who shaves everyone who does not shave himself," we are still acting as if the classification is rigid and not man-made. When the man is shaving other people his classification becomes "man who shaves other people." When he shaves himself, he belongs to another category, "man who shaves himself."… We must remember that all these classifications are arbitrary and man-made and should be changed when the thing classified or its use changes.

This is a great illustration of how we treat a word as a real thing. The paradox does not exist if you see past the idea of barber as a rigid thing that exists-in-the-word and is attached to a thing, as some kind of physical label, and instead see it as an arbitrary definition. If you focus on what you observe, there is no paradox.

This is an important part of what general semantics is all about – distinguishing between words/symbols and what's-out-there. In some cases, it would almost be better not to use words to gain understanding. We will have more to say about this later.

But back to the idea of logical destiny: If you accept a certain premise, a certain conclusion follows. And if your premise or assumptions are not valid, you will reach a false conclusion – unless you accept an inconsistency.

The Investment Implications of Future Events Are Unknowable – Even When You Know the Future!

Here is an example from the marketplace where a seemingly logical assumption fated you to a doomed conclusion. It comes from Michael O'Higgins, the president of O'Higgins Asset Management, an independent, fee-based investment advisory based in Miami. In a July 2016 blog post titled "If We Had a Crystal Ball," he posed an interesting question about gazing into that crystal ball.

He asks you to suppose that on January 31, 2006, you knew with certainty that the price of gold would more than triple over the next five years, from $569 per ounce to $1,900 per ounce. Knowing that, might you have invested in Newmont Mining, the world's second-largest gold producer?

Odds are high that you would have gladly bought Newmont shares. With that kind of surge in the price of gold, buying shares in one of the world's largest gold companies would seem like a no-brainer.

Yet, the share price of Newmont fell 5% over that time.

The premise was wrong: A rising gold price doesn't mean gold mining shares go up. Gold mining shares are businesses. They have costs. They have financing needs. The stocks have valuation multiples, subject to all the whims of the market. A rising gold doesn't automatically lead to a rise in the price of Newmont shares.

O'Higgins ran through several other examples…

Suppose that at the start of 1973 you knew that the earnings of the Dow Jones Industrial Average would rise 50% over the next two years. Seems you would bet on the Dow, right?

Well, the Dow got cut in half.

The premise: rising earnings lead to rising stock prices. Wrong. Again, too many real world variables were left out of the premise. The valuation on those earnings could fall, for example, as they did.

Say you could know ahead of time which companies would make money and which would lose money. You'd likely invest in the former. In 1999, the stocks of companies that actually made money declined 2%. Profitless tech startups soared 82%.

Premise: Stocks of companies that make money do better than stocks in companies that lose money. Not so. At least, not all the time…

And here's one more example.

"In 2016," O'Higgins wrote in July of that year, "Brazil's senior leadership has been embroiled in a vast corruption scandal, President Dilma Rousseff's powers have been suspended due to impeachment proceedings, Finance Minister Joaquim Levy has been forced to resign, and inflation is in double digits. Brazil suffered its worst GDP contraction since 1990."

If you had known all that was going on, you probably would've stayed away from Brazilian stocks. Yet, the Brazil iShares ETF was up nearly 60% through July.

"Even if we had a crystal ball," O'Higgins concludes, "the investment implications of future events and conditions are unknowable." (Remember this next time you hear one of those market pundits telling you what the future holds.)

But there are other kinds of logic that can trip us up, too. What if I say:

If A is better than B

And B is better than C

Then A is better than C.

Would you agree?

It seems entirely logical. In fact, this kind of reasoning has a name: the transitive rule. Ed Thorp writes about this in his book *A Man for All Markets: From Las Vegas to Wall Street, How I Beat the Dealer and the Market.* As he notes, you can replace "better than" with "longer than," "heavier than," "older than," "more than," or "larger than," and the rule is true.

"However, some relationships don't follow this rule. For instance, *is an acquaintance of* and *is visible to* do not."

Remember the game rock, paper, scissors? That's non-transitive. Scissors beat paper, paper beat rock, rock beat scissors. There are also non-transitive relationships in voting preferences and in consumer preferences, which can lead to seemingly irrational choices.

The point here is not to be seduced by seemingly impeccable logic. If you question premises, the soft points in any argument will reveal themselves.

Often, in markets and in life, the underlying premise is based on nothing more than the idea that the past is prologue – or the idea that relationships that held in the past will hold in the future.

I distinctly remember hearing, before the financial crisis of 2008-09, that "housing prices never go down." The idea was based on the empirical fact that before the crisis, national housing prices had never gone down significantly since the Great Depression. Whether that was actually true or not is beside the point; it became a meme that helped the housing bubble reach enormous proportions.

All you had to do was question the premise. Are you thinking as clearly as you might when you believe that because something hasn't happened before, it can't happen? Was it so hard to create a scenario where housing prices could collapse, especially given a seemingly steep rise in prices compared to other factors such as income?

Scott Adams, the cartoonist, brilliantly lampooned the kind of backward-looking thinking that believed housing prices could never fall. In his column "The Odds of Being Killed By an Immigrant," Adams wrote:

> I keep seeing tweets and articles saying the odds of an immigrant killing a citizen of the United States are approximately zero. Obviously those calculations assume that our past experiences do a good job of predicting what happens next. And this is good news. Really, really, good news.

> It's good news because I used to be afraid of lots of stuff that never happened in the past. For example, I have never died from a nuclear attack, but now I understand that risk to be zero. We can dismantle our nuclear deterrents and relax. If a nuclear bomb hasn't killed me in the past, I can safely conclude that it will never kill me in the future.

Logical fate (or logical destiny, if you prefer): Remember the concept and be sensitive about what premises you accept. The fate of your conclusions hangs in the balance!

Key Takeaways

- Logical fate means certain conclusions follow inevitably from certain premises. Therefore, it is important to be critical of and examine your premises.

- You can reach a perfectly logical conclusion that is nothing but nonsense because your premises were off. Remember the shortcomings of GDP and what it purports to measure.

- The barber's paradox shows you how words can bind our thinking by creating a false premise.

- False premises are more common than you might think. For example, that gold prices rising means gold stocks go up. We looked at a great example from Michael O'Higgins that shows, in dramatic fashion, how such a premise could've cost you a lot of money.

Chapter 7

The Difference Between a Fact and an Inference

Imagine you hold an apple and say: "There are seeds in this apple."

Is that a statement of fact? Or is it an inference?

Knowing the difference between a fact and an inference is an important idea we will explore in this chapter. It seems basic, but as you will see, you know far fewer facts than you think. By the end of this chapter, I hope I'll have convinced you that's true.

I once gave a presentation on this topic for which I shamelessly borrowed from the great Irving J. Lee (1909-1955). I gave him credit at the time and will do so again here.

Lee was a professor of public speaking at Northwestern University. He wrote a book called *Language Habits in Human Affairs*, published in 1941. I have the original hardcover, in which Korzybski wrote the foreword. Lee was one of Korzybski's best students.

On YouTube there is a great presentation by Lee called *Talking Sense* from 1952, which I must've watched three times and which inspired my presentation. I talked about the difference between a fact and an inference, which was a distinction Lee sought to make in his talk.

So far in this book, we've talked loosely of 'facts.' But facts are quite rare in the scheme of things.

I began my presentation by talking about an apple, just as Lee did, even using most of his phrasings verbatim:

> I picked this up at the grocery store. It's an ordinary apple. I haven't tampered with it. Now suppose you say: "There are seeds in this apple."
>
> The question I want to ask you is: "Did you make a statement of fact?"
>
> You might say: "Well of course, that's a statement of fact. There have been seeds in all of the other apples I've ever dealt with. Every time I've ever cut open an apple there have been seeds in it. So far as I am concerned, that's a statement of fact."

Now… I would like to cast some doubt about that. I would like to ask you to wonder whether that is actually something you know.

And if you say this is a statement of fact, I want to ask you whether you are thinking as carefully as you should.

I then ran through a magic trick using a matchbox, which was slightly different than the trick Lee performed. I emptied the matchbox in front of the crowd and closed the box. I then continued:

Suppose you say: "The matchbox is empty."

I would ask you again: "Did you make a statement of fact?"

One way to think about it is to ask yourself how confident you are in that statement. Would you be willing to bet on it?

I don't know what you'd say, but I'm guessing you'd be fairly confident it's empty. Maybe you're not 100% sure, because you're probably getting suspicious about what I'm doing here…

Well, that's good.

I'd like to again cast some doubt about what you think you know.

As with the seeds in the apple, I'd like you to think about whether the box being empty is something you really know. Is it something you can be sure about? Or is it something that seems very, very likely?

Of course, I had actually slipped a penny into the box using an old sleight-of-hand trick. But the point was to get people to think about what they really know versus what they think is likely.

Irving Lee's Schematic for Separating Facts From Inferences

I continued, channeling Lee:

In English, we can make what people call a declarative statement. We are taught that a declarative statement asserts a fact. There are seeds in this apple. The matchbox is empty.

These are declarative statements. However, none of these are statements of fact. I would like to suggest that we distinguish between a fact and an inference.

An inference is a guess, hunch, reckoning, opinion, belief, supposition... by inference I mean any of those words.

Lee had a neat little schematic that I shared with the attendees. It shows you the difference between a fact and an inference:

Fact	Inference
• You can make a statement of fact after you observe something	• You can make anytime
• Stays with what can be observed	• Goes beyond what can be observed
• Is as close to certainty as we can get	• Involves degrees of probability

Summing up, I said:

In other words, I can take this apple, and I can say it's round; I can talk about its color, or how much it costs, and so on... These are things that can be observed.

But if I say there are seeds in this apple, I go beyond what can be observed. I can't see whether there are seeds in this apple. To do that, I have to cut open the apple.

Another way to think about it, as for certainty that there are seeds in this apple: Would you bet your life? I wouldn't.

The odds are very great, and it's very probable... but you can't be certain.

It's probably obvious to you now that there isn't all that much we know for certain. As investors, we deal mostly with inferences. Therefore, it may help us to think in terms of a continuum. On one end is near certainty – 'facts,' as we call them. And on the other end of the spectrum are wild guesses. In between

How Do You Know?

lie varying degrees of certainty. This mirrors more closely the real world, as all inferences are not equal; some are better than others. (And we don't want to get too hung up on our own definitions, which are arbitrary anyway.)

Thinking in this way brings a few ready benefits:

- It's harder to be dogmatic. If you are less sure of what you know and are less enamored with what other people call 'facts,' then you are less likely to get stuck asserting something that turns out not to be true.

- You are more likely to change your mind, as you are more open to the idea that you can be proved wrong. The great fear of many investors is that they become so wed to their 'facts' that they can't see when they are wrong. Bill Ackman provides what is perhaps a famous case study here, where he rode Valeant down more than 90% from its peak even as his thesis crumbled.

- You are more open to expect the unexpected. After all, if you have no particular commitment to inferences – understanding their limitations – you are open to the idea that new observations can better them, or provide a surprise.

We can't help but make inferences. I do not want to leave you with the impression that we should not make inferences, or that we should not rely on them.

What Inferences Can You Rely On?

There is a metaphor about this that I like from cognitive scientist Donald Hoffman. Think of your computer and the icons you see on your screen. These are the things you see. They are the only things you can assert about anything on your desktop – the color, shape, position, etc. of those icons. Yet none of them tell you anything about what goes on inside the computer.

As Hoffman says, "You could not form a true description of the innards of the computer if your entire view of reality was confined to the desktop. And yet the desktop is useful. [It] guides my behavior, and it hides a complex reality that I don't need to know."

In a sense, you use your computer based totally on inferences and with no observational or factual knowledge of the inside workings of your computer at all.

When I made my speech, I was at a hotel in Delray Beach, Florida. I inferred that the stage upon which I spoke would support my weight. I also inferred that the roof would not collapse on me and that the water provided would not kill me. I could not verify all these things ahead of time. However, these inferences were high-quality inferences, you might say.

Therefore, this brings us naturally to the idea of standards. What standard will you use to verify your 'facts'? This is actually a complex question. Let us run through an example inspired by a very similar one Weinberg used in his book.

Suppose there is a table. You use a tape measure and declare it is 30 inches high. Is that a fact? It would seem so, but... on what standard?

Suppose a friend came along with an electronic instrument accurate to 1/1000th of an inch. He declares the height of the table is actually 30.019 inches. Is that a fact? And does that mean that your measurement is no longer a fact?

Of course, you could get even more 'accurate' measurements. Even then, you'll run into problems. Eventually, you get down to the molecular level. Then you find that your sharp-edged table is actually a cloud of ever-moving molecules – and where is the edge of a cloud?

Weinberg writes:

> What, then, is the 'real' height of the table? Our answer is that there is no such thing. It is a meaningless question because, as of this date, there is no possible way, actual or imaginable, to arrive at an answer. The table is 30 inches high. The table is 30.019 inches high. Both are correct; both are accurate; both are factual statements. Nor do they contradict, for two different standards are used.

Which standard you select depends on what you are doing. For most purposes, the 30 inches from your tape measure is good enough. But we could imagine more scenarios where we'd need more exacting standards.

The other lesson here is that observation alone may not establish a fact. We need to know by what standard. If someone told you the table was 30 inches high, your next question would be, "How do you know?"

All Statements About the Future Are Inferences... But So Are Statements About the Past

When you really sit and think about this stuff, even things you might take for granted you start to question, or at least hold with a softer grip. For example, all statements about the future must be inferences by nature. You can't observe the future. But all events about the past are also inferences – except those based on actual observation by you (or the speaker or writer as the case may be).

This gets a little difficult to understand at first. After all, this means that when you sit down and read history, you're reading a collection of inferences. History is a mixture of guesses, hunches, based on evidence of varying grades of quality selected by the historian and similar evidence rejected by that historian who is, let us not forget, a fallible human being with a reality tunnel that colors all he or she sees (and doesn't see). Thus, things you normally would say in knee-jerk fashion are 'facts' are, on closer inspection, inferences.

There is a famous story involving professor Weinberg that illustrates this point well. He was teaching a course in general semantics in the 1960s. On the day of our story, he was trying to get his students to understand the difference between a fact and an inference, as we've just done.

At one point, he offered his class the following example: "Fact or inference: John F. Kennedy is president of the United States."

The class shouted, "Fact!"

And Weinberg said, "No!" He pointed out again the difference between a fact and inference, using the same basic schematic as Irving Lee's that I used above. "We've all been in class for almost an hour. Who's to say as a matter of fact that John Kennedy is president of the United States? It is an *inference*, although a highly probable one. He might have resigned, his back pain may have incapacitated him, he might even have been killed. Such a statement is *not* one of fact."

As the story goes, class ended shortly after noon. The date was November 22, 1963. And the students all learned, in a visceral way, what Weinberg meant to teach them.

Getting mixed up and believing your inferences without question can have serious consequences. ("Suppose the Trojans had checked that wooden horse?" Weinberg asks.) Much of the drama around literature and movies hangs around some kind of faulty inference.

But now so armed with the ideas in this chapter, you too will be sensitive to the differences between facts and inferences. You will be more careful about what you know and what you assume.

Lee in his "Talking Sense" speech told a wonderful story involving President Eliot of Harvard, about this idea of being careful about what you assume and what you know:

> Eliot entered a crowded NY restaurant and handed his hat to the doorman. After lunch, he goes to leave.
>
> As he came out he was astonished to see the doorman promptly pick out his hat from the hundreds that were there and hand it to him.
>
> "How did you know that hat was my hat?" Eliot asked.
>
> "I didn't know it was your hat, sir," said the doorman.
>
> "Why, then, did you hand it to me?"
>
> And the doorman very courteously replied, "Because, sir, you handed it to me."
>
> President Eliot was delighted with this precise delimitation of what the doorman saw and what he assumed.

That is the kind of thinking I have been trying to cultivate in myself and in which, through this book, I am trying to impart on you.

Key Takeaways

- We explored the difference between a fact and an inference.
  - Fact:
    - You can make a statement of fact after you observe something.
    - Stays with what can be observed.
    - Is as close to certainty as we can get.
  - Inference:
    - You can make anytime.
    - Goes beyond what can be observed.
    - Involves degrees of probability.
- There isn't much we know for certain, but understanding this leads to a number of benefits:
  - It's harder to be dogmatic.
  - You are more likely to change your mind, as you are more open to the idea that you can be proved wrong.
  - You are more open to expect the unexpected.

Chapter 8

Words Don't Have Meanings; People Give Them Meanings

"A Japanese man went into a bank to change some Japanese notes into sterling. He was surprised at how little he got.

'Please explain,' he said to the cashier. 'Yesterday I was changing same yen for sterling and I received many more sterling. Why is this?'

The cashier shrugged his shoulders. 'Fluctuations,' he explained.

The Japanese man was aghast. 'And fluck you bloody Europeans too,' he responded, grabbed the notes, and walked out."

~ Richard Oldfield, *Simple But Not Easy*

"You can never hear one word from anyone... You hear only your own translations always. They are all your words you are hearing."

~ U.G. Krishnamurti

For the 500 most used words in the English language, the *Oxford Dictionary* lists over 14,000 meanings.

This is not surprising on reflection. It has to be that way. After all, there are a near infinite number of things 'out there' and possible ideas we could describe. And yet we deal in a limited inventory of words, even if we include the expanded vocabulary of specialized disciplines.

In this short chapter, we will see why this is an important idea and how it can hinder our ability to make accurate "maps"...

So, given a limited inventory of words, there are always things that remain outside the purview of our language, but just because we cannot describe them or don't have a word for them does not mean these things do not exist. As Alan Watts put it, "For a society whose number system is only '1, 2, 3, many,' it cannot be a fact that we have ten fingers, and yet all the fingers are visible."

This hard reality militates against clear communication and sets the groundwork for many a debate. Two investors may debate whether XYZ Industries is a good business or not, but often the debate arises because the two debaters simply have a different idea about what makes a 'good business.'

I remember watching a debate between two economists, Warren Mosler and Robert Murphy, from two different schools of thought. And at one point they got into a debate over the so-called 'natural rate of interest.' As I had fairly deep knowledge of the theories of both schools, I could see clearly what they – and the moderator – apparently could not see: Each school defined 'natural rate of interest' in a different way. As a result, they weren't so much debating as simply talking past each other, over a definition – which enlightened no one.

And how many times have you taken it for granted that when someone uses the terms 'earnings' or 'free cash flow' that they mean what you mean when you use those terms... only to find out later that they meant something quite different?

The idea that words have some mystical correct definition cannot square with the reality of our situation – a near infinite number of things and a far smaller set of words to affix to them. People give words meaning. Words themselves have no intrinsic meaning. Words are pliable; they bend to the will of those who use them. And the meanings that have currency at any one time shift and change as well.

Thus, we should take the physicist P.W. Bridgman's advice:

> Never ask 'What does word X mean?' but ask instead, 'What do I mean when I say word X?' or, 'What do you mean when you say word X?'

And my corollary to this would be:

> Don't automatically assume that when someone else uses a word, they mean it to mean exactly what you think it means.

Obviously, you can take this to stupid extremes. As a practical matter, we can't go around asking everybody what every word they use means. And besides, even if you did that, you'd quickly realize that you'd only be pushing back the problem one degree. Because really you'd have to ask them what the words in their definition mean, and what the words in their definition of their definition mean, and so on ad infinitum. You would never get anywhere.

It's like using the dictionary. You look up a word to find the definition of a word. You find the definition uses more words. If you look up the definition of those words, you find more words. There's no end to it... which is itself an interesting find.

This leads to the second important insight of this chapter:

> All human knowledge is circular. All of our thoughts/feelings rest ultimately on indefinable terms.

We'll have more to say about this when we talk about the silent level in a future chapter. For now, it's enough to know that words are just words. At some point, to show what a word really means, you have to point to something.

Bruce Kodish uses the example of a horse. If you ask what a horse is, there are two ways I can answer you. I can give you a definition with words – basically, something out of the dictionary. Or I can take you out to a pasture or a racetrack and point one out to you.

In general semantics, we call the first definition an *intensional* definition; and the second we call an *extensional* definition. I know the language is a little awkward, but if you want to go on and read other books on general semantics, you'll want to gain some comfort using these terms. (In Part II, we will go over some tools to help you think extensionally.)

The idea, or one idea, of general semantics is to get you to think more in extensional terms. Most people readily think in intensional terms. You ask them what something 'is' and they're quick to give you a verbal description or definition. But that definition – that map, if you will – leaves things out. And sometimes what's left out may be essential.

Korzybski gives us a memorable example in *Science and Sanity* of the two definitions using the word 'house':

> The dictionaries define 'house' as a 'building for human habitation or occupation,' etc. Let us imagine that we buy a house; this buying is an extensional activity, usually with some consequences. If we orient ourselves by intension we are really buying a definition, although we may even inspect the house, which may appear desirable, etc. Then suppose we move into the house with our furniture and the whole house collapses because termites have destroyed all the wood leaving only a shell, perhaps satisfying to the eye. Does the verbal definition of the

house correspond to the extensional facts? Of course not. It becomes obvious then that by intension the term 'house' was over-defined, or over-limited, while by extension, or actual facts, it was hopelessly under-defined, as many important characteristics were left out. In no dictionary definition of a 'house' is the possibility of termites mentioned.

In markets, it does not take much imagination to see where you could go wrong relying on intensional definitions. We've already seen numerous examples in this book to back this point: an entertainment and leisure ETF full of airlines (and no Disney), a homebuilder ETF with non-homebuilder stocks, and companies with "dot com" in their name that were not really internet properties, etc.

It may be impossible to be purely extensional, and you wouldn't want to be. Both definitions have their uses. But it does seem our society skews heavily toward the intensional definition. And you can see clearly where extensional thinking would be an aid to clarity.

Almost all of our labels are intensional as such. When we describe a stock as a biotech, utility, bank, retailer, miner, insurer, or media company, we rely on intensional definitions. But we have all run across stocks that have a certain label but functionally are closer to something very different.

"A change in language can transform our appreciation of the cosmos," the linguist Benjamin Whorf once said. And he was right, as we will soon see in an upcoming chapter on the "Whorf-Sapir Hypothesis."

Favor Concrete Language

"No one can be conscious of abstracting all the time, not even me and I wrote the book!"

~ Alfred Korzybski

Careless inattention to big, abstract words may have helped foster the worst financial crisis since the Great Depression of the 1930s, as Harold Evans contends.

Evans edited *The Sunday Times* and *The Times* of London. In 2001, his peers voted him the greatest British newspaper editor of all time. In 2004, he was knighted. In 2017, at the age of 88, he published *Do I Make Myself Clear? Why Writing Well Matters.*

The book is well worth your time if you do any writing at all. But for our purposes, Chapter 10, titled "Money and Words," holds a provocative thesis. It gets to the heart of why language matters.

Evans maintains that the Great Recession – that epic bust of 2008, the worst crisis since the Great Depression of the 1930s – had roots in words "to an extent not commonly appreciated." There was "no common name and no comparable scrutiny for the new banking beasts in an unpoliced jungle inhabited by a wild menageries of money managers who borrowed short, lent long, and repackaged risky loans as bonds."

Words performed their magic and held people in their spells. "Triple-A" meant safe. But few dug behind the simple words and definition to get at the thing itself. CDOs (collateralized debt obligations), SIVs (structured investment vehicles), monoline financial guarantors, credit derivative products, etc.... Or the idea that, as we mentioned before, "housing prices never go down."

As *The Washington Post* reported:

> Countless delusions and mistakes brought on our financial crisis, but none did as much damage as the belief that home prices never go down.
>
> People have long seen real estate as a safe investment. The notion is intuitive – the supply of land is limited, and the population is always growing – and until 2007, national home prices had not fallen significantly since the Great Depression.

A whole constellation of words, ideas, and concepts seduced and deceived millions of people. No one was quite sure what it all meant, even those who should have been in the know (investment advisors, regulators, central bankers, etc.).

Evans quotes Gillian Tett, a *Financial Times* journalist:

> Professional experts wield power precisely because they wrap their craft in language that is labeled the preserve of "geeks." It is hard to start a public policy debate if there are no widely accessible words to explain the ideas being conveyed.

If people had tried to pierce the veil of words (those maps) and get at the territory, perhaps the bubble would have been averted sooner. Perhaps it would never have reached the scale it did and the damage would not have been as great.

How Do You Know?

Instead, people relied on history ("housing prices never go down"). Mathematical models ruled the day. As Evans puts it: "An obsession with words, and the meanings behind the gobbledygook, would have been more appropriate, given how many acronyms were time bombs."

Books such as Evans' help you tighten up your writing, but they also help clarify your thinking. Another book on that front I like is *The Writer's Diet: A Guide to Fit Prose* by Helen Sword. This slim volume aids you in weeding out abstractions and replacing them with concrete nouns.

Concrete nouns refer to things we can see, touch, taste, smell, or hear. Abstract nouns express intangible ideas "remote from the world of the human species." As Sword puts it, "We can talk and think and argue about *sadness* and *affection* and *reciprocity*, but these concepts bear no physical weight."

Naturally, fuzzy thinking tries to take refuge in abstractions. You will need to root them out. Sword gives an example of how an author attempted to hide his weak reasoning in abstract language:

> MRCD [Multirecursive Constraint Demotion] can be applied to a set of full structural descriptions, and it will either determine that the set is inconsistent or return a grammar consistent with all the descriptions. **This** means that we could try to deal with structural ambiguity by collecting a set of overt forms, and from each overt form generate all possible interpretations of the form. [Bold italics in Sword's original.]

Sword highlights that sneaky "this." What does it mean? What does it refer to? "Here," Sword writes, "*this* serves as shorthand for 'the fact that MRCD can be applied to a set of full structural descriptions,' or perhaps for 'the fact that MRCD will either determine that the set is inconsistent or return a grammar consistent with all the descriptions.'" The author buried his intention instead of stating it clearly, perhaps with good reason.

Whenever you encounter a "this," Sword advises, "ask yourself, 'This *what*?'" If it is not clear what "this" means, you may have found a problem.

In the business world, we encounter abstract language all the time. Take this description of what a company does, from the company itself: "[XYZ] designs, procures, and executes branded marketing materials and retail experiences for the world's leading brands."

This example is not the worst I could find. But it's typical, loaded with abstractions. What are "marketing materials"? And what does it mean to "execute" them? Why not just be specific and say "we design, procure and make advertising flyers, signs, and billboards." And how about that term "retail experiences"? That's like flying a big flag saying, "We're trying to make it sound like we do something way more impressive than what we actually do."

Favor concrete language. When you find it missing, ask questions. People tend to hide things behind abstractions. Don't assume people use words to mean what you think they mean.

Key Takeaways

- Words don't have meanings. People give them meanings.

- From this flow many important corollaries. Among them: Don't automatically assume when somebody uses a word, they mean it exactly as you mean it.

- All human knowledge is circular in that all of our thoughts/feelings rest ultimately on indefinable terms.

- We talked about the difference between extensional and intensional meaning.

- The dictionary definition is intensional; the showing or pointing is extensional. General semantics aims to get you to think more extensionally as an aid for clarity of thought.

- Concrete language refers to things we can see, touch, taste, smell, or hear.

- Abstract language expresses intangible ideas such as greatness, fairness, equality, etc.

- Naturally, fuzzy thinking tries to take refuge in abstractions. Favor concrete language.

Chapter 9

A Tango: Questions and Answers

"How come you have so many questions? I am not giving any answers."

~ U.G. Krishnamurti, *The Courage to Stand Alone*

In the spiritual world, there are gurus, and they attract followers who come to them with questions. The guru sits on a chair with an audience before him. He may give a short talk, and then he takes questions. This can go on for hours. It is called a satsang.

In finance, there are similar performances. The Berkshire Hathaway annual meeting is akin to a satsang. Warren Buffett and Charlie Munger sit up on a stage and take questions for hours.

It can be frustrating sometimes, sitting in that audience, because the questions some people come up with make you want to hit them over the head with a wet towel. Perhaps there are no stupid questions. But there are meaningless questions. In this chapter, we explore the nature of questions.

Just because we put a question mark at the end of a series of words doesn't mean we have something that we can answer, or should. As Bridgman pithily put it: "I suspect that a good deal of philosophy has had its origin in the endeavor to find verbally satisfactory answers to questions that sounded as though they ought to have answers."

Let's take an example from Korzybski, which he borrowed form Einstein. Take anything, say, a pencil. Let us say that the temperature of this pencil is 60 degrees. Now consider this question: "What is the temperature of an electron that makes up part of this pencil?"

Some may answer "60 degrees." Some may answer, "I don't know." But as Korzybski pointed out, these answers are both senseless because they try to answer a meaningless question. "Temperature by definition is the vibration of molecules... so to have temperature at all, we must have at least two molecules." The term temperature does not apply to a molecule split into atoms.

That is a rather esoteric scientific example, but it makes the point. And we could come up with something else in finance. For example, let's consider a company that lost a lot of money. Consider the question: "What is the price-earnings ratio of its stock?"

We can come up with a number. It would be a negative number. But it would be meaningless. The correct way to answer the question would be to say, "The question doesn't make sense, because the company did not have positive earnings and therefore a price-earnings ratio is meaningless."

As someone who for years wrote a newsletter that anyone could buy if they plunked down the $49 subscription fee, I can tell you I've seen a lot of bizarre questions from people who probably should stay far away from investing their own money.

For many unsophisticated investors, a price-earnings ratio is the primary valuation tool they use. But they do not understand the nuances and limitations of it.

Hence, I get a well-meaning question such as this: "Could you establish a general all-inclusive P/E for the recommended portfolio?"

I could, but what good would it do? The underlying assumption is that a price-earnings ratio would be a meaningful statistic for a diverse portfolio of businesses that includes financial stocks, banks, retailers, and conglomerates.

A price-earnings ratio for such a portfolio would be meaningless. Say we have a two-stock portfolio. The price-earnings ratio of the bank stock we own is 12 and the price-earnings ratio of a fast-growing tech name is 30. The average is 21. So what? It means nothing. The two companies are very different. You can't average unalike things in this way. It's an abuse of math. You can't take the price you paid for an apple and the price you paid for a car and expect an average of the two to mean anything. It's the same with stocks.

The idea here is that we need to think about our questions before we try to answer them. Remember we talked about logical fate? The same holds true here. If you ask a poorly structured question, you won't get a good answer.

As a society we spend a lot of time on how to give answers. We spend less time learning to formulate a question.

To start, we need a way to sort different types of questions.

A Typology of Question Types

Robert Pula, a general semanticist we've heard from several times in this book, suggests a simple typology.

The four categories are:

- Operational/extensional
- Speculative
- Fun
- Pathology-inducing/intensional

Operational/extensional questions are ones that we can readily get an answer to. "How do I drive from the Willard Hotel in Washington, D.C., to the Marriott Waterfront in Baltimore?" Well, we can look that up and find the answer.

"What companies are competitors of General Motors?" We can answer that question. "What did the S&P 500 return in 2016?" Again, we can find an answer. These are useful types of questions, the workaday questions. But there are other questions that are of a different kind altogether.

Once, I gave a presentation about the virtues of long-term investing. I talked about the power of compounding. I talked about ignoring the short-term fluctuations in the market. I talked about the folly of forecasting.

And when I was all done, the very first question I got was this – and I am not joking: "What is your outlook for the next six months?"

I have many adjectives I might use to describe this question in this context. At the moment, I'll just say this is an example of a question that is not operational/extensional because it deals with the future. I can't get the answer. It is a speculative question, and a silly one at that.

Speculative questions are those that have no reliable answers. Investors spend an inordinate amount of time and energy thinking up these questions and trying to answer them. Stop spending so much time trying to figure out where the market is going to go, or what interest rates are going to do, or what the Fed's next move is.

And yet…

Not all speculative questions are so horrible. We need speculative questions, because they can lead us on a path to other questions. Maybe we ask ourselves, "Gee, shipping stocks are down 90%. Have we hit bottom in the shipping industry?" Now, we can't know that for sure without the benefit of hindsight. It's a speculative question. But it may lead us to do more work on shipping stocks and fish around for 'value' there.

It pays to know what speculative questions are. Answers to such questions should not get the same weight in your mind as an extensional question. Yet, again, in my long newsletter career, I see readers give equal weight to both speculative knowledge and more extensional knowledge (or down-to-earth knowledge) all the time.

For example, they will take a bearish forecast on the stock market by some guru and treat that as nearly a fact. Thus, I'll get a question along the lines of: "So and so said the market was going to crash this September. Shouldn't I wait before I buy XYZ?"

Well, my thesis on XYZ is based on a lot of research and a readily identifiable anomaly that gives us a chance to pick up a dollar for 50 cents. The crash call for September is one of four dozen such calls in the last 10 years by the same guy and is based on a seeming prejudice of the forecaster against stocks as such. Yet, the reader, as his question shows, weighed both equally.

Fun questions are kind of self-explanatory. "Who would win in a fight, Superman or Batman?" The intent here is play. "These are perhaps the most healthy questions of all," Pula writes, "because they generate little negative tension... and practically any answer will do."

Investors, too, ask playful questions, "What would you do if you had to invest a million dollars today and not touch it for five years?" Or those questions people will ask on Twitter such as, "Which stock will appreciate the most in 2018: Wal-Mart or Amazon?" It's just a fun thing to talk and wonder about. Even asking, "What do you think the market will do this year?" can be a fun question if the intent is such.

Finally, the pathology-inducing/intensional questions. These are questions that come from, in Pula's analogy, "the darkest cave... unlit by *consciousness of abstracting*." Included here would be questions that assume assertions of paranoia. Pula gives an example: "'Why is that man looking at me that way?'"

I get questions along these lines, too, usually from people who exhibit extreme fears of government: "If the government is going to confiscate IRAs, why should I buy this stock in my IRA as you suggest?" There are many variations on this theme.

I would be even broader minded than Pula here. "What will GDP for the second quarter be?" That's speculative, because it's about the future, and we can't get an answer. But I also think it's pathology-inducing unless the person asking it realizes that GDP is an abstraction. That is, GDP doesn't exist. It is a guess. And what does it really have to do with anything practical you might do today?

Any question that is not conscious of the abstracting going on could potentially be pathology-inducing.

Wendell Johnson explores this idea further in his book *People in Quandaries*. Maladjusted people, he contends, spend a lot of time trying to answer unanswerable questions. "Why did this happen to me?" "Am I a failure?" "Am I happy?" "Why am I here?"

We torture ourselves unnecessarily by asking questions we cannot answer. "It is an unnecessary torture," Johnson writes. "It comes about as the result of a semantic trick. It can be avoided by the simple means of not asking – or of not trying to answer – unanswerable questions."

Or we pretend we know a lot more than we do and answer questions – often assertively – about things we should probably stay quiet on. When I'm asked about what policy I'd recommend for trade or immigration or health care or whatever, I usually cheerfully answer that I don't have one. Why should I? Why do we feel we should have opinions on political matters of the moment? Why must we have sorted out opinions on what other people regard as 'important'? Why can't we leave a thing unanswered, unsorted out?

And is the presumption underlying most policy discussions defendable? I am reminded of anthropologist David Graeber's "against policy (a tiny manifesto)," found in *Fragments of an Anarchist Anthropology*. He writes, "Policy is by definition something concocted by some form of elite, which presumes it knows better than others how their affairs are to be conducted." An enormous arrogance underlies all policy discussions.

Our fellow human beings have a way of creating problems so they can provide a 'solution.' We can't even rest now without doing so with the idea that it should be "deliberate rest" – rest that will stimulate our productivity and thinking somehow. See, for example, *Rest: Why You Get More Done When You Work Less* by Alex Soojung-Kim Pang. ("Rest is a skill," writes the author. Ay yi yi.)

The Soldier and the Hunchback

The above typology of questions is a simple sorting system, but I think it's helpful. As investors, focus on those operational/extensional questions. That's where you get your bang for your buck, so to speak. Answers from those questions should be more reliable than answers to the other types of questions. Most people spend too much time formulating speculative questions, such as asking about a six-month forecast.

Aleister Crowley is one who thought a good deal about the nature of questions. He wrote an essay called "The Soldier and the Hunchback" in 1909. As strange and baffling as his writings often seem, he is a bit of a linguistic philosopher at times. His thinking on questions and answers is largely compatible with the one we outline here. To wit: "Answer is impossible if you ask: Are round squares triangular? or Is butter virtuous? or How many ounces go to the shilling? For the 'questions' are not really questions at all."

In his essay, the hunchback is a metaphor for a question mark, which the punctuation mark's outline vaguely resembles. The soldier represents an exclamation point, a soldier standing straight, at attention. And, among other things, Crowley points to the seemingly never-ending series... ?!?!?!?!?

There are, in other words, no final answers. Every answer begs more questions. And the hunchback and the soldier continue in a never-ending tango. But that is part of the fun of the game – as long as we don't torture ourselves over questions with no answers.

—

Key Takeaways

- Just because we put a question mark at the end of a sentence doesn't mean we have a question we can answer, or should answer. There are meaningless questions.

- We need to think about our questions before we try to answer them.

- We looked at four different types of questions: operational/extensional, speculative, fun, and pathology-inducing/intensional.

  - Operational/extensional are questions that have readily findable answers.

  - Speculative questions do not have answers now, but may have answers in the future.

  - Fun questions are questions where the intent is playful. These are harmless.

  - Pathology-inducing/intensional are questions for which there are no answers.

- We torture ourselves unnecessarily by asking questions we cannot answer.

Chapter 10

The Whorf-Sapir Hypothesis

"Human beings do not live in the objective world alone, nor alone in the world of social activity as ordinarily understood, but are very much at the mercy of the particular language which has become the medium of expression for their society. It is quite an illusion to imagine that one adjusts to reality essentially without the use of language and that language is merely an incidental means of solving specific problems of communication or reflection. The fact of the matter is that the 'real world' is to a large extent unconsciously built up on the language habits of the group. ... We see and hear and otherwise experience very largely as we do because the language habits of our community predispose certain choices of interpretation."

~ Edward Sapir (1884-1939), anthropologist-linguist

The linguist Benjamin Whorf (1897-1941) had an interest in Mexican antiquities and lore. In particular, he studied the Aztec language and Mayan hieroglyphs. He formulated a useful hypothesis for our project about how our language impacts what we see and think. We will explore his idea below.

First, a little about Whorf the man...

The label "linguist" seems inadequate to describe what Whorf did. He worked for the Hartford Fire Insurance Company for most of his working life, where he was by all accounts quite successful. In between, he worked as an independent scholar, where his output, at times, was greater than what you'd expect out of a full-time professor. Much like Korzybski, he followed his own curiosity and contributed immensely to the field in which he worked.

As a boy, Whorf had an interest in Mexico's pre-history, in its ancient temples and mysterious hieroglyphs. He read William Prescott's *The Conquest of Mexico* several times. But he had wide interests, including botany and religion and the language of other Native Americans, such as the Hopi. As an adult, his studies and papers brought him in contact with the leading scholars of his day in archeology and linguistics.

In 1930, he took a field trip to Mexico, where he collected archeological data and made a number of discoveries. In the course of his short life – he died of cancer in 1941 at the age of 44 – he contributed many path-breaking and incisive papers. Whorf's amateur status has sometimes been used by his critics as a way of dismissing him, but as Stephen Levinson writes in his foreword to a collection of Whorf's writings titled *Language, Thought, and Reality*:

> Amateurism is not the right gloss for a man who published three or four scholarly papers a year, often in the top journals of his profession, taught at Yale, enjoyed the regard of the leading scholars of his day, and contributed enduring terminology to the discipline. Like Darwin, Whorf simply preferred the comfort and independence of his own means.

Whorf's reputation has risen and fallen in a cyclic pattern over the years since his death. Following the path of these arguments would take us too far afield. I would simply recommend, as a great starting point in studying Whorf, the book mentioned above edited by John B. Carroll, Stephen C. Levinson, and Penny Lee titled *Language, Thought and Reality: Selected Writings of Benjamin Lee Whorf*. This edition includes an informative foreword by Levinson and a 42-page introduction by Carroll that deals with Whorf's work in a wider context as well as his critics.

Whorf's ideas attract debate because, as Levinson notes in his foreword, they are "a seductive, revolutionary set of ideas." The idea he is most known for today is that language itself has an impact on what we think.

The Linguistic Relativity Principle

This idea he called the "linguistic relativity principle." In his words:

> [This] means, in informal terms, that users of markedly different grammars are pointed by their grammars towards different types of observations and different evaluations of externally similar acts of observation, and hence are not equivalent as observers but must arrive at somewhat different views of the world.

The idea of linguistic relativity is open to various interpretations. We won't go into the idea in any great depth here, but you'll find a summary of some key ideas useful.

Whorf studied the work of Edward Sapir, a contemporary anthropologist and linguist. (Whorf would teach Sapir's graduate seminar on Native American linguistics at Yale while Sapir was on sabbatical.) In a paper Whorf wrote in 1939 called "The Relation of Habitual Thought and Behavior to Language," he led off with a quote from Sapir. (You'll find it at the start of this chapter.)

In this paper, Whorf has some interesting examples he pulled from his work at Hartford Fire. Whorf studied hundreds of reports on how fires got started. He saw that sometimes a "linguistic meaning" had a role to play.

He wrote about gasoline drums, which, so labeled, were handled with great care. However, when labeled in the mind as "empty gasoline drums," people tended to get careless. The drums are empty, after all. Yet empty gasoline drums are perhaps more dangerous because they contain explosive vapor. He fingered the linguistic meanings embedded in the word "empty," which suggest a "lack of hazard," among other things.

Another example is the way people behaved around "limestone." Because it had the word "stone" in it, people took little care to protect this material from excessive heat. In one episode, it caught fire and "to everyone's great surprise burned vigorously."

Another time, Whorf found a tannery that discharged wastewater in an outdoor settling basin partly roofed with wood. A worker, thinking it "a pool of water," lit a blow torch and threw his match in the "water." But the gas emitted from the pool lingered under the roof and the flare of flame ignited it, the woodwork, and eventually, the adjoining building.

Whorf writes:

> Such examples, which could be greatly multiplied, will suffice to show how the cue to a certain line of behavior is often given by the analogies of the linguistic formula in which the situation is spoken of, and by which to some degree it is analyzed, classified, and allotted its place in that world which is 'to a large extent unconsciously built upon the language habits of the group.'

Sapir and Whorf became most associated with this idea that language impacts thought, hence the idea became known as the Sapir-Whorf hypothesis.

Korzybski, our epistemological knight-errant, found much that he liked in Whorf's work. Korzybski recognized Whorf's work (and to some extent Sapir's) as a non-Aristotelian orientation. They had come to similar conclusions about the connections between language and behaviors/perceptions. Korzybski, in fact, came to these ideas in the 1920s, a decade before Whorf published his findings.

(See Robert Pula's paper, "The Nietzsche-Korzybski-Sapir-Whorf Hypothesis?" Pula shows how Nietzsche also had similar ideas, which would predate even Korzybski. Pula suggests renaming the hypothesis the Nietzsche-Korzybski-Sapir-Whorf Hypothesis to, as he says, "straighten out the chronology.")

Korzybski invited Whorf to speak at the Second American Congress on General Semantics held in Denver in August of 1941. Whorf died that July, though, and his paper was read at the Congress.

There is little doubt Korzybski thought the hypothesis had merit. He included the idea in his last paper, "The Role of Language in the Perceptual Processes." He wrote:

> We do not realize what tremendous power the structure of an habitual language has. It is not an exaggeration to say that it enslaves us... and that the structure which a language exhibits, and impresses upon us unconsciously, is automatically projected upon the world around us.

Enslaves us. Strong stuff. If we aim to clarify our thinking, we must realize the hold language has on us and not let the embedded assumptions pass unexamined.

Key Takeaways

- We looked at the ideas of Benjamin Lee Whorf, in particular his "linguistic relativity theory."

- Though open to various interpretations, the basic idea is that language impacts our thinking.

- Whorf uses examples from his work in fire insurance to show how language and its embedded assumptions influenced people's behaviors (for example, "empty gasoline drums" that were, in fact, more dangerous than full ones).

How Do You Know?

Chapter 11

The Silent Level

"Civilization is a conspiracy of noise."

~ John Zerzan

"All I ever wanted

All I ever needed

Is here in my arms

Words are very unnecessary

They can only do harm"

~ Depeche Mode, "Enjoy the Silence"

The artist Marina Abramović once gave a performance at the Museum of Modern Art in New York in which she sat in a chair with a table in front of her and another chair opposite her. People in the audience would come up, one at a time, and sit in front of her… in silence.

No words were ever spoken by Marina or her onlooker, but many people had emotional experiences. As Silvia Jonas wrote in a piece for *Aeon* titled "Unspeakable things":

> Some laughed; many cried. Arthur Danto, the late Columbia University philosopher and art critic, compared his time with Abramović to 'a shamanic trance', and described the show as 'magic' in *The New York Times*. More than 1,500 people came and sat with Abramović, and 750,000 attended as observers. A recurring sentiment among the visitors was that the performance was a deep revelation for which words were not sufficient. If this is true, then something about it was ineffable.

Indeed, there is something about the unsayable, the silent level – or what Korzybski called the "unspeakable objective level." This is where we live. This is where we have our primary experience. It comes before speech. In this chapter, you'll see the benefits of tapping this silent level.

You may recall, in an earlier chapter, our discussion of the structural differential. Flip back to the picture of that model. You can see in that model how our first verbalizing of the "Event" is an abstraction, strained of countless details.

I'll say it again: You need to know that the verbal world is not the world out there, an idea which gets to the heart of non-A orientations generally.

The word "chair" is not the thing you sit in. The "stock" is not the company out there in the real world with people and assets and customers and debts, etc. If you stub your toe, you feel certain sensations. If you put those into words, you cannot capture those sensations. The words will be different; they are not the experience. As Korzybski said, "Whatever you say it is, it isn't." The 'map' is not the 'territory.' The 'menu' is not the 'meal.'

We can put lots of things into words but not capture the thing itself. Jonas, in her *Aeon* piece cited above, offers her own example: She knows how to play the violin. But if she tried to verbalize how to play the violin, you would not be able to play it yourself as a result of listening to her. There is an acquired 'know-how' at the unspeakable level that you only gain through experience.

"Similarly," she writes, "I could try to explain the colour red to you, in terms of the latest scientific theories about wave-lengths, retina receptors and human colour-perception. But no matter how comprehensive my description, *phenomenal knowledge* can't be passed on through language."

Jonas mentions the philosopher Thomas Nagel's famous paper, "What Is It Like to Be a Bat?" Her reference made me re-read it. Nagel makes the case that it is impossible for us to gain a real understanding of what it is like to be a bat. Bats perceive the world in a way we can only describe with words – such as describing how sonar works.

Try as we might, we can't experience what it is like to be a bat. "If I try to imagine this," Nagel writes, "I am restricted to the resources of my own mind, and those resources are inadequate to the task." Again, we can talk about a bat. But we can't experience what a bat experiences.

In fact, we don't need to talk about bats. We can talk about people. None of us experiences the world in quite the same way. You can watch a movie or read a book or witness an accident or value a stock… and your view will be different than someone else's in many ways, sometimes in critically important ways.

And putting that full experience into words is impossible. You can only fall short. For example, this is a real review of a beer posted on the site BeerAdvocate, and it is by no means atypical:

> Nice spotty soapy lacing clings down the glass, with a moderate amount of streaming carbonation retaining the cap. Aromas of lemon, ginger, pear, apple, wheat, cracker, honey, brown sugar, toasted oats, biscuit, herbal, floral, pepper, grass, and yeast earthiness. Nice and pleasant aromas with good balance and complexity of fruity yeast, pale malt, honey, molasses, and earthy hop notes; with solid strength. Taste of lemon, ginger, pear, apple, wheat, cracker, honey, brown sugar, toasted oats, biscuit, herbal, floral, pepper, grass, and yeast earthiness. Light-moderate herbal/grassy/spicy bitterness on the finish; with lingering notes of lemon, pear, apple, wheat, cracker, honey, brown sugar, toasted oats, biscuit, herbal, floral, pepper, grass, and yeast earthiness on the finish for a good bit.

Yeah, sure. That's a lot of words – a lot of rich, descriptive words. And yet, I still have no idea what this beer tastes like. I never will know just by reading about it, no matter the talent and skill of the writers. The only way for me to know is to drink it myself.

This may seem obvious, even perhaps a little silly. Yet, it is easily forgotten that what we say about a thing/experience is not the thing/experience. It is an abstraction.

Most importantly, it is easily forgotten that there is value in that silent, or nonverbal, level.

Understanding You Can Only Grasp Non-Verbally

Korzybski was not the first to recognize this. Zen, for example, is all about the unsayable. (And several writers have noted the affinity between Zen and general semantics.) Zen teaches liberation by "pointing," using puzzles (kōans), not analysis and discussion.

"The fundamental position of Zen is that it has nothing to say," Watts wrote in *Psychotherapy East & West*. "The blue hills are simply blue hills / The white clouds are simply white clouds." There is an understanding that is beyond the verbal level, indeed that can only be reached nonverbally.

This means, perhaps, that this chapter will be short...

Seriously, though, the main idea here is simply to think more about what is happening than how we describe it. This is extremely hard to do. As U.G. Krishnamurti – a thinker we will hear more from later – pointed out, it is hard to look at anything without right away trying to put it in words. "Red bag, table, chair, hard, soft! That is you, nothing else," he says. "You are a collection of memories, definitions. You never once look without telling yourself what it is you are looking at!"

You can find this out for yourself. Try this exercise from Bruce Kodish:

> Spend the next few minutes letting sounds from your surroundings come to you. Notice any tendency to label what you hear or talk to yourself in any other way. How well can you put aside these labels and bring yourself back to the sounds? ...

> Eventually one can begin to construct these kinds of sensing experiments and ask sense-able questions for oneself. There are endless experiments to do. Sensory awareness can be done anywhere, anytime: while waiting in lines, for a bus or in traffic, sitting in a lecture or at your computer keyboard, etc.

Trying to stay silent is a lot harder than it sounds. I urge you to try it.

I like to go for long walks or jogs. And I've tried at times to just absorb the sights and sounds around me without verbalizing internally what I see and hear. It is hard. But there is a benefit to the exercise.

For one thing, I've learned you appreciate how much is going on – you pick up on sights and sounds you otherwise pay no attention to. You start to look at the world with a sense of wonder. Experiencing the silent level in this way also makes it easier to absorb and understand the ideas in this book. You know the word is not the thing, at a visceral level.

General semanticists in the Korzybskian tradition have long been fans of the silent level. Irving Lee dedicated a chapter in one of his books to it, titled

"When to 'Keep Still.'" He succinctly summed up the benefit of the silent level: "An understanding of this silent universe will help dissolve the false-to-fact character of our limited, too-often dogmatic talk."

It's easy to talk. It's harder to be silent. It's harder to just 'take things in.' The world out there is far richer and more complex than our language can convey. And it is limiting to label something and let those labels dictate what you see and think.

The inability to see past labels is why most people will never reach a real understanding of anything, never mind investing.

As a writer on various financial topics related to investing for many years, I can tell you that editors and publishers like to tell us writers that we need to tell our readers what to do. You can't just make observations, or write a thoughtful piece that arrives at no real conclusion. You have to give the reader an action to take.

But the need to be told what to do is precisely the reader's problem. They are looking for answers, always looking for someone to tell them what to do. And so they bounce around. They try this approach, then that one, always looking, looking, looking...

There are no final answers! Once you realize there are no final answers you can just be, take things in, absorb... not label, not fit things into your box, not jump to conclusions using some approach you learned second hand. What you need is primary experience. Something that is yours...

Silence Transcends Speech

"Silence is so accurate."

~ Mark Rothko (1903-1970), painter

Sages and wise men have long known the value of silence. It's a cultural cliché: the bearded holy man on the mountain sitting in deep meditation.

Ramana Maharshi (1879-1950), the famed Indian teacher of the last century, often sat in silence when people visited him at his ashram. Much like with Abramović, visitors would have powerful experiences in that silence. But such experience doesn't require any mystical faith. Ramana Maharshi was wise to the ways of the world, and there are many quotes I could share that fit with the core ideas in this book. For example:

Q: What is reality?

A: It is not with forms and names. That which underlies these is the reality. ... It transcends speech."

Ramana Maharshi asked, "How does speech arise?" First you have to abstract from the reality you perceive around you. This gives rise to a thought, which in turn becomes a word. Ramana Maharshi used to say, "the word is the great-grandson of the original source."

Korzybski would've approved.

Key Takeaways

- Sometimes it's better to just keep quiet. Silence can convey more than words ever can. As Lee said, "An understanding of this silent universe will help dissolve the false-to-fact character of our limited, too-often dogmatic talk."

- By silent level, we also mean trying to quiet our thoughts and resist labeling and coming to conclusions about what we sense and feel.

- The world 'out there' is always more than we can convey in words.

How Do You Know?

Part II
Devices for Clear Thinking

How Do You Know?

Prelude

Some Basic Propositions

"A great many of our human troubles are only artificial verbal bubbles, and when they are pricked they burst so there is nothing left but to laugh."

~ Alfred Korzybski, General Semantics Seminar 1937

Now, for Part II, we're going to focus on practical ways to use the ideas we've covered so far.

Before we do that, I offer the following basic propositions, which build on everything to this point:

1. Our world changes continuously; nothing stays the same

2. No two things exist exactly alike

3. Observer and observed create what the observer sees

4. We can never know all the details; we always leave things out

I like these so much I advise tacking them near your workspace somewhere. I find they help keep your thinking straight while you're doing your research on stocks or just reading about companies and the world.

In what follows, we'll look at different tools to use that deal with each of these four propositions.

Chapter 1

Dating

"What I say today may be correct, for tomorrow I don't know. Dogmatism and absolutism are abolished permanently by the use of dates. If you make a statement with great security and if you date it, you have no 'cosmic legislation' for tomorrow."

~ Alfred Korzybski, General Semantics Seminar 1937

Our world changes continuously; nothing stays the same. This is the first of our propositions.

This ancient wisdom seems to need little proof. Heraclitus, the Greek philosopher, said you could not stand in the same river twice. He recognized the river would be different each time, as water flows, depths change, the course changes, stuff that floats and moves with the flow of the water changes, etc. Change was central to Heraclitus' worldview. "Everything changes and nothing stands still," he wrote. Even rocks, mountains, seas… all change over time.

Even something like your desk changes slightly from minute to minute. It may look like the same desk, but if you left it there for 20 years, you'd see the effects of an aging process. It didn't happen overnight.

Nothing remains the same.

Despite the seeming obviousness of this, investors have made the opposite view the epitome of wisdom. Thus the old phrase attributed to John Templeton: "The four most expensive words in the English language are, 'This time it's different.'"

Investors will frequently mock or deride a case for an investment by using Templeton's phrase, "This time is different," in a sarcastic way. As if to say, "You nut, don't you see this is the same basic pattern we've seen before? This time is no different!"

Of course this time is different. This time is *always* different. And every time is always different from every other time. Episodes may seem similar on the surface or in certain important ways, but there are countless details that are different from prior episodes. And you cannot be sure those details don't matter. To blithely wave them away with a snarky reference to Templeton's maxim seems foolish at best.

We live in a world in process. As Irving Lee wrote:

> The winds, the rains, and the snows; the ebb and flow of the waves and currents of the sea; the shifting clouds; the rhythm of the seasons ceaselessly changing; the growth and aging of animals and men... these are but a hint of the gross changes we perceive about us, an ever so brief list of the endless and sometime haphazard flux of our "restless universe."

In the world of people and culture, things change, too. Even you yourself are a process. "I am" implies an unchanging thing, but an "I" is really a process. As R. Buckminster Fuller (1895-1983), an architect and designer, put it, "I seem to be a verb."

Change is inherent in our world. Fashions come and go. Laws change. Scientific knowledge evolves. Industries rise and fall. Widely accepted ideas make way for new widely accepted ideas. 'Biological realities' dissolve into new 'biological realities.' (People used to accept the four humors as a 'biological reality.' Humorism dominated Western medical practice for centuries. But nobody gives such theories any credence today.)

Newspapers were once great businesses. They are no longer. New businesses that didn't even exist 15 years ago, such as Uber, disrupt industries and destroy older business models. Shopping and spending habits change. The list goes on and on.

Alan Watts used the example of a university. For example, consider the 'University of Maryland.' We call it that as if it is a stable identity. But students, faculty, administrators and even buildings come and go. The 'University of Maryland' is itself a process, always changing.

Investor Thomas Russo likes to give another analogy. He talks about visiting a 700-year-old temple in Japan. It is made of wood and none of the wood is 700 years old, as pieces have been replaced multiple times over the years. But we talk about the temple as if it is 700 years old.

In markets, we see the effect of change in many similar ways. Consider the S&P 500, one of the most frequently cited market indexes. Did you know that prior to 1976, there were no financial companies in the index? In 1976, Standard & Poor's changed the rules and replaced 60 companies in the index, adding financials. There were also major changes after the dot-com bubble burst in 2000, in which 56 companies were swapped out. On average, over the last 50 years, 20-plus companies are swapped out each year.

Yet, investors cite and treat the S&P 500 as if it were a monolithic, unchanging thing. But it clearly isn't, as a look at the top weights in the index by year show.

In 2000, the top 10 looked like this (with market caps in billions):

- General Electric, $474

- Exxon Mobil, $302

- Pfizer, $290

- Citigroup, $287

- Cisco, $275

- Wal-Mart, $237

- Microsoft, $231

- AIG, $229

- Merck, $215

- Intel, $212

In 2017, they looked like this:

- Apple, $736

- Microsoft, $501

- Amazon, $422

- Exxon Mobil, $338

- Johnson & Johnson, $338

- Facebook, $402

- Berkshire Hathaway, $401

- JPMorgan, $300

- General Electric, $257

- Google, $574

That's a lot of big changes. The S&P 500 of 2000 is not the same as the S&P 500 of 2017, even though our language infers that it is. We say, "The S&P 500 trades at a premium above its 10-year average." But the S&P 500 today is different than the S&P 500 of 10 years ago, five years ago, etc.

We even treat the companies as if they were the same. But Berkshire Hathaway of 2016 is markedly different than the Berkshire Hathaway of 2000.

In 2000, Warren Buffett led off his shareholder letter this way: "Our gain in net worth during 2000 was $3.96 billion, which increased the per-share book value of both our Class A and Class B stock by 6.5%."

And his five largest investments were American Express, Coca-Cola, Gillette, *The Washington Post*, and Wells Fargo. His total stock portfolio was $10 billion.

He led off his 2016 letter this way: "Berkshire's gain in net worth during 2016 was $27.5 billion, which increased the per-share book value of both our Class A and Class B stock by 10.7%."

The first thing that strikes you, of course, is the size. Berkshire in 2016 was a lot bigger than Berkshire in 2000. And his stock portfolio? In 2016, it came to $122 billion, not $10 billion. The top holdings were: Wells Fargo, Coca-Cola, IBM, American Express, and Apple.

More importantly, Berkshire has evolved over the years into more of an operating company that generates earnings as opposed to an investment company that generates dividends and capital gains.

The point is Berkshire Hathaway 2016 is not Berkshire Hathaway 2000.

This is the basic idea behind our first device: dating.

Put a Date on It

What Korzybski advised is that you use a date. It's so simple. When you write Berkshire Hathaway, you date it like this: Berkshire Hathaway$_{2017}$. That makes it clear that you are referring to the Berkshire of 2017. It is a little mental reminder that Berkshire Hathaway$_{2017}$ is a thing that changes. You could even be more precise and say Berkshire Hathaway$_{April 14, 2017}$, because companies can undergo meaningful change in the course of a year.

Big acquisitions, buybacks, divestitures, new products and announcements, etc. all can have a big impact such that Whole Foods at one date is different enough from Whole Foods even one day later.

When you write about or refer to any company or stock, date it. When you write about or refer to the S&P 500, date it.

Now, you may think this impractical. And perhaps it is. But, at least mentally, do it. Really try to internalize this and you will see some interesting results.

I remember once speaking with a hedge fund manager who worked at Blackstone, the famous asset management firm and widely respected as a firm of "smart guys." We were talking about names we thought were interesting. I threw out the idea of Vivendi, the French media conglomerate. This is a company that had undergone massive changes in just a few years. For example, there had been major divestitures, which resulted in a company that had net debt turning into one that had a large pile of excess cash.

But this Blackstone manager seemed unaware of it. He made passing reference to Vivendi's indebted balance sheet. I knew then that we were talking about different companies. I was talking about Vivendi$_{2017}$. He was talking about a Vivendi that existed at least a few years before. He had not looked at the name recently, and it showed.

If he had followed Korzybski, he would've at least mentally dated his knowledge. Thus, he might've prefaced his comment by saying, "I haven't looked at Vivendi since such and such a date…"

Perhaps more importantly, you catch yourself from making such errors. You know when someone tells you something interesting about AIG$_{2016}$, you don't make the mistake of thinking AIG$_{2016}$ is the same as AIG$_{2008}$ – when it was a mess and got a bailout from Uncle Sam.

I see readers of mine do this all the time, as I've mentioned before, and it causes them to make obvious mistakes and close off certain ideas because they harbor outmoded thoughts about it. Readers chafed at the idea of investing in AIG$_{June\ 2016}$ because they couldn't get AIG$_{2008}$ out of their heads. But AIG$_{June\ 2016}$ proved a good investment and was up 34% by the end of the year.

This works well with people, too. My view of Bill Ackman$_{2014}$, when Pershing Square returned a net 40% gain to investors, is quite a bit different than my view of Bill Ackman$_{2015}$ after Valeant – the notorious pharmaceutical company – collapsed and his fund delivered a net loss of 20%.

By dating my thinking, I set a reminder that Bill Ackman is not the same every year. And also important, by dating, I see that it makes no sense to have a commitment to my view. Just because I thought Ackman was a great investor in 2014 does not mean I have to stand by that view today.

This same logic works wonderfully for countries, objects of any sort, ideas, statements, etc.

This is what Korzybski meant when he said dating would abolish "dogmatism and absolutism." Part of the idea behind general semantics is to use language that better fits the world as it is. By dating, we explicitly recognize our world as an ongoing process. It flows, like Heraclitus' river. It's always changing.

Key Takeaways

- Our world changes continuously. Nothing stays the same. We explored the implications of this simple observation.

- We think about the S&P 500 as if it is a monolithic, never-changing thing. But, in fact, the composition of the S&P 500 changes markedly over time, which begs the question of how useful it is to compare the S&P 500 today to the S&P 500 in years past.

- Companies change as well. The point is Berkshire Hathaway 2016 is not Berkshire Hathaway 2000.

- Thus, our first device: dating. If you date statements, things, etc., it reminds you of their place in time. For example, 'Berkshire Hathaway$_{\text{April 14, 2017}}$.'

- This doesn't mean you have to actually go around dating everything with subscripts. But you should mentally date them and recognize they are point-in-time observations.

Chapter 2

Indexing

"Once more we can get a bit of wisdom from the mathematical method. I believe it was the great mathematician Sylvester who said that 'in mathematics we look for similarities in differences and differences in similarities,' which statement should apply to our whole life orientation."

~ Alfred Korzybski

No two things exist exactly alike. Yet, in investing and in life, the language we use often strongly implies otherwise.

We seem to do this frequently with people. We'll refer to 'immigrants,' 'Muslims,' 'consumers,' 'truck drivers,' 'Wal-Mart employees,' 'brokers,' and on and on. We use these classifications thoughtlessly, not considering if there is an established norm of some kind that makes the classification meaningful.

Robert Anton Wilson gives us vivid examples as to why this underlying assumption is not warranted. In this case, he uses the words 'male' and 'Jewish':

> You can no more find the male norm from Gandhi, Bozo, Gen. George Custer, Buddha, Bill Clinton, Louis Pasteur, Osama bin Laden, Kung Fu Dzu, Bruno, Father Damien, Michelangelo, Mozart, Ted Bundy, etc. than you can find the Jewish norm from Emma Goldman, Harpo Marx, Felix Mendelssohn, Spinoza, Barbra Streisand, Nathaniel Brandon, Emma Lazarus, Jerry Seinfeld, etc.

When you adopt a non-A orientation, you see that the common idea of a 'norm' simply disappears.

We've already dealt with some of the most obvious ways we do this in financial markets. For example, the way we talk about 'stocks' as if they were all the same. The way we talk about specific classifications, such as coal stocks, obscures many important differences among the stocks we blanket with such a category, differences that manifest in widely varying performance.

Korzybski gave us a simple tool to remedy this: the index.

This is something he took from mathematics. You may remember using symbols such as x_1, x_2, and x_3. This is a mathematician's way of showing that the variable 'x' can be one number in one instance and another number in another instance. In other words, x_1 does not equal x_2. (I realize subscripts have other uses in mathematics, but for our purposes, this is the relevant usage.)

Likewise, when we say, "She is a fundamentalist, just like Jane," we should realize that "fundamentalist$_1$" does not equal "fundamentalist$_2$." They are different. Using an index allows you to still recognize both as part of a classification ('fundamentalist') but not smother the individual identity of each.

Horowitz writes eloquently about this, and I quote him here:

> The formulation "she is a fundamentalist," without indexing, *forces* our attention exclusively onto what (we think) all fundamentalists have in common as members of the class. The index is Dr. K's gentle soothing remedy, guiding our attention to *this* fundamentalist here, whom we can hear, see, etc. with who we can converse, emphasize, etc. The index politely invites us to relate to *this* one in her specificity... And to revise and enrich our concept of fundamentalist.

The index pushes back on our tendency to make sweeping generalizations about a class or category. Instead of allowing the generalization to pass unquestioned, the index flags it. Whatever we may say about a person generally by making a deduction based on a classification, we know nothing about this person specifically.

We use indexing extensively already in many areas of life. We use them in house numbers. Not just a house, but house number 14. Not just any driver's license or phone, but this specific license number and this specific phone number.

What general semanticists propose is to use indexing whenever we talk about classifications or categories. Remember, a core idea behind general semantics is to be conscious of your abstractions and your abstracting, to be aware of your generalizations. Practice with the index helps the idea seep deeper into your psyche. Eventually, thinking this way will become second nature.

Then you won't make such a mistake as assuming acre$_1$ equals acre$_2$, which is what investors in real estate and natural resource companies do all the time.

St. Joe is a classic example of how this mistake occurs. St. Joe is a real estate company based in Florida. It owns over 600,000 acres of land in Florida in the panhandle region around Destin. Some of this is along the Gulf of Mexico and includes miles of beachfront property.

Investors made a bullish bull case for the stock that depended on the valuation of those acres. Here is one example of the thinking at work, one of many examples I could pull:

> At a market cap of $3.6 billion, the market is valuing its land at about $5,700 an acre. That's a huge discount. Some of that land was selling for over $250,000 an acre a year ago. So you know the company is way undervalued using a net asset value method.

Do you?

What's the mistake this analyst makes? With indexing, it is obvious. The underlying assumption is that $acre_1$ equals $acre_2$. Thus, you can take the land that sold for $250,000 per acre and impute a value on the rest of the 600,000-plus acres.

But is that fair to do? In 2010, David Einhorn, of Greenlight Capital fame, presented St. Joe as a short – meaning he was betting against it – at the 2010 Value Investing Congress, which I attended. In part, his thesis relied on highlighting the simple fallacy in the bullish argument. He showed how some of St. Joe's rural land was worth as little as $900 an acre. That's a far cry from $250,000 an acre.

If our bullish analyst had used indexing, he might've written: "Some of that $land_1$ was sold for over $250,000 an acre…" This would've alerted him that $land_1$ doesn't equal $land_2$, or $acre_1$ does not equal $acre_2$. Instead, he might've tried to think more about individual acres and what they might be worth. *This* acre, not some mythical average, or imputed, acre. And he might've avoided his costly mistake.

The stock, which was $40 in 2008, was $17 in 2017 – almost 10 years later. This wasn't the only error the bulls made, but it was a big one.

Investors made the same mistake with figuring out the value of acreage with oil and gas firms. Here's a classic example, where an analyst is making the case for SandRidge Energy. The analyst shares a number of transactions where SandRidge sold some of its acreage in Mississippi.

Then he writes:

> The Mississippian acreage that SandRidge still retains, roughly 1.5 million acres, has an implied value of some $6.35 billion. If you add up the proceeds from the sale of that 550,000 acres and the current value of its retained acreage, you get roughly $8.7 billion. That's $3.5 billion more than the company's current enterprise value – from just one play alone!

You can see he commits the same error as our St. Joe bull. He equates $acre_1$ to $acre_2$. Once again, a little indexing would've prevented him from committing this thinking error.

Now, this stock went to zero – a bankruptcy, as the whole energy complex went into a bear market and prices collapsed. So, it may be unfair to single out this error, as the stock was doomed in any event. But, certainly, the use of indexing here would've dampened the analyst's enthusiasm and might've prompted a deeper look.

As Horowitz points out: "Without the index, it is easy to lie with statistics."

The Chain Index

So, that's the value of the index. There is an extension of the index called the chain index. What this does is put the subject in an environment, or a context. Things do not exist in a vacuum.

As indexing reminds us, $fish_1$ is not the same as $fish_2$. But $fish_1$ in water is not the same as $fish_1$ on a platter. In this case, using a chain index we might write instead $fish_{1 \text{ in a fish tank}}$ to differentiate it from $fish_{1 \text{ grilled on a platter}}$.

Another example: A friend of mine is an otherwise flexible thinker when we talk about investing. He is willing to consider varying points of views, to look at different angles, to consider different narratives, to explore ideas without dogmatic commitment.

But he drops a bunch of IQ points when talking about politics. When it comes to his politics, his point of view is affirmed by "biological reality" (a favorite phrase) and "accepted by science" and "backed up by facts." His thinking becomes remarkably rigid. The transformation is quite striking. $Friend_{1 \text{ talking about investing}}$ is not $friend_{1 \text{ talking about politics}}$.

This reminds me of Wilson's observation that "belief is the death of intelligence." He wrote, "As soon as one believes a doctrine of any sort, or assumes certitude, one stops thinking about that aspect of existence." The more certain you are, the less there is to think about.

The chain index reminds us that the thing is not even the same as itself in different environments and contexts. You are not the same person at work as you are at home. A CEO in front of a group of investors is not the same CEO in front of his direct reports. Irish War Cry, a thoroughbred racing horse, is not the same at the Kentucky Derby as at the Preakness. Phil Mickelson is not the same golfer at the Masters as he is at the Open.

Your phone in New York City is not the same in French Polynesia where you get no service. The way we use language, though, encourages us to think there is this thing called "my phone" that exists as a thing-in-itself. But things work differently in different environments. Your phone, technically, is never simply your phone. It is always your phone in a given location – and at a specific time. This is why Horowitz says, "whatever is indexed should also be dated." The simple reason is that there is no being (or thing) outside of time.

As investors this extends to businesses and products. Coca-Cola in Mexico is not the same as Coca-Cola in the U.S. In this case, Coke actually has a different formula for Mexico and Latin America. A Big Mac in Tokyo is not the same as a Big Mac in Rio.

Perhaps investors overlooked this point when they bid the shares of Arcos Dorados to such a premium valuation at its initial public offering (IPO) in 2011. The stock opened at $21 and soon hit almost $29 per share. Arcos Dorados is the sole Latin American franchise for McDonald's. And the number of McDonald's restaurants in Latin America was just a tiny fraction of what was in the U.S. Investors got excited.

But McDonald's in, say, Brazil, is not McDonald's in the U.S. In Brazil, McDonald's food is not cheap for locals (as it is in the US), and this is largely true throughout Latin America. And so the whole dynamic of what McDonald's is changes. Risks were also different, as Arco Dorados was operating in countries with many different currencies.

Investors were slow to see these differences. It was a costly mistake. The stock lost 90% of its value to a low in 2015 of $2 and change. McDonald's in North America is not McDonald's in South America.

Belief systems differ in context, too. "There are as many different Islams as there are situations that sustain it. And they can all be classified as Islam," Horowitz notes. Value investing as taught at Columbia University is not value investing as Marty Whitman teaches it in his books.

When we take animals and put them in cages, they are different than what they were in their own natural habitat. When we take people and study them in lab-like settings – whether testing drugs or taking polls – they are not the same as the people they are outside of those settings. People lie to pollsters, after all, and the questions asked can affect their answers.

Indexing everything may seem like a lot to ask. I hardly expect you to go around literally adding little subscripts to everything with an index, a place, and a time. But mentally, you should. At least, you should think about it.

I would like to conclude this section on indexing with an observation by professor Lee. He said it is a mark of sophistication to see differences.

For example, let us say I set out a table with various bottles of wine. I might look at them and simply say: "I see several bottles of red wine." But a more sophisticated observer will see differences. The sophisticated observer will know something of the different flavors among the wines and might know the different regions they've come from or something about the wineries.

Or consider two golfers. One is an amateur and the other is a club pro. The amateur might simply see the fairway and obvious markings, such as trees and traps. The club pro will note far more details – slopes and wind – and will think ahead to setting up the second shot.

It is, as professor Lee said, a mark of an uneducated person – of the unsophisticated, the amateur, the tyro, the untrained person – to not see the differences.

In fact, what we mean by training is someone who can see the difference – a golf pro, a wine expert... or an investing pro who knows all stocks are not the same, and appreciates differences among companies in the same business and even the same company at different times and places.

But when you see only differences or similarities, you get into trouble...

Professor Lee taught: It is the mark of the mature mind to see both. Aim to see similarities among things that are different and see differences where the unsophisticated see similarities.

Key Takeaways

- No two things exist exactly alike.

- Yet, we rely on classifications and categories where we treat everything in that category as if it were the same ('stocks,' 'Americans,' 'consumers,' etc.).

- Korzybski suggested the use of an index to remind us individuals (or units) in a category are not the same.

- So, as we saw in the case of valuing St. Joe, a land company, $acre_1$ does not equal $acre_2$.

- Further, the use of a chain index reminds us a thing is not the same as itself in different environments and contexts. $Fish_{1\ in\ a\ fish\ tank}$ is not the same as $fish_{1\ grilled\ on\ a\ platter}$.

Chapter 3

Korzybski's Pencil, Etc.

"Remember the Etc."

~ Irving Lee

Recall that the map is not the territory. Meaning the word is not the thing, the narrative is not the event, etc. We can never know all the details; we always leave things out.

You can see this if you look back at Korzybski's structural differential, which we looked at in Chapter 1 of Part I. The structural differential shows quiet clearly how we leave out details as we make sense of the world around us. We can never capture everything. In general semantics, we call this the principle of non-allness, which is an important principle of non-A systems.

In contrast to non-allness, there is the principle of allness. You can detect the latter when you hear or read words such as *all, everyone, nobody, never, every*, and *absolutely*, among other terms. ("Everyone agrees..." "Nobody believes..." "Every stock..." "Never buy this...")

Allness can also be implied, such as in the statement: "Airlines are bad businesses." The natural reaction for someone with a non-allness orientation would be: "All airlines? All the time?"

Or another such statement I heard recently, "Foreigners don't get rich in China." Again, the natural comeback here is, "No foreigners of any kind? Ever? Under any circumstances?"

What we want to do is cultivate an awareness of non-allness. Such awareness will naturally raise questions in the face of allness-type thinking. It makes obvious our tenet that we can never know all the details; we always leave things out.

A favorite example used by general semanticists to illustrate this principle is what I'll call Korzybski's pencil. I've found the metaphor alluded to in a few different books. (We mentioned a pencil before, but that was in a different context. It seems Korzybski had a fondness for using pencils as a teaching tool.) It makes the point in a memorable way, and so I'll reproduce it for you here.

Korzybski wrote:

> Let us take any actual object; for instance, what we call a pencil. Now, we may describe or "define" a "pencil" in as great detail as we please, yet it is impossible to include *all* the characteristics which we may discover in this actual objective pencil. If the reader will try to give a "complete" description or a "perfect" definition of any actual physical object, so as to include "all" particulars, he will be convinced that this task is humanly impossible. These would have to describe, not only the numerous rough, macroscopic characteristics, but also the microscopic details, the chemical composition and changes, submicroscopic characteristics and the endlessly changing relationship of this objective something which we have called pencil to the rest of the universe, etc., an inexhaustible array of characteristics which could never be terminated. In general, physical abstractions, including daily-life abstractions, are such that *particulars are left out* – we proceed by a process of forgetting. In other words, no description or "definition" will ever include all particulars.

Try as you might, you can never describe 'all' of a pencil. Now, you may read the above example and say, "Who cares? It's a pencil, for crying out loud." And yes, this is a trivial example. But it makes an important point, and we can readily imagine more serious instances.

For example, what about reading news coverage of different events? Think about the last U.S. presidential election pitting Donald Trump against Hillary Clinton. Did Fox and CNN cover the candidates in the same way? Or did they each leave out different things? How about *The New York Times* compared to Breitbart?

If you hold to the principle of non-allness, you'll know they are all leaving things out. As Horowitz put it, "the media of the 'right,' the 'left,' the 'center,' etc. are gigantic selection/deletion machines, programmed to leave out much information that would not support their pre-established framings."

This is true of investment research as well. When an analyst recommends a stock, he tells you all the good things about it. He probably will not spotlight the negatives in the same way. He may be well-meaning, but he's human. Likewise, a short seller, looking to take down a stock, will emphasize the negative. Even if both were completely well-meaning and wanted to be even-handed, they could not be. It is impossible to represent all, as the example of Korzybski's pencil reminds us.

How Do You Know?

We may *know* that we can't know or describe *all*, but we often don't act that way. A bullish report on a stock, which otherwise has no new information, can boost the stock the day of its release. When Bill Ackman presented the Howard Hughes Corporation as his stock idea at the Sohn Conference 2017, the stock jumped almost 4% that day. Yet, this was a stock Ackman had owned for years – a fact that was well known. And he said nothing new. Yet, people easily forget the principle of non-allness.

For that reason, Korzybski suggested a useful reminder. He suggested we use "etc." (as in "etcetera," meaning, "there's more here than I'm saying," or "more could be said"). Thus, you might say, in the case of Korzybski's pencil: "This pencil is yellow with a nick on it and a worn-down eraser and is about 5 inches long, etc."

Or thinking of things we use grapes for, you could say: "We use grapes to make wine, juices, etc." Or you could describe a business such as Berkshire Hathaway: "It owns insurance companies, railroads, Coca-Cola, etc."

The little "etc." is a powerful reminder that we're leaving things out. It may seem too simple, but if you use it, you'll see the effect it has as it works its way into your thinking. As Horowitz says, the etc. "is an explosive device: it blows 'closure' or 'totality,' invoking the non-A principle of non-allness."

Korzybski himself referred to etc. as "junior infinity." The "etc." is a useful tool. I recommend it to you. Be liberal with your etceteras, at least in your mind if not in the spoken and written word.

More Tools: Sombunall and "So Far as I Know"

Robert Anton Wilson coined the word "sombunall" to stand for "some but not all." It was another way to cultivate an awareness of non-allness. "Sombunall Irishmen are drunkards," as he wrote.

Wilson suggested that anytime you hear the world "all," you stop and think about it. "Is 'all' the right word here? Do we know enough? Does 'sombunall' fit the facts better?" It is hard to be dogmatic, or assert much of anything emphatically, if you can't generalize. Thus, sombunall has a way of forcing you to keep an open mind.

I think it's safe to say sombunall hasn't caught on. But I like it nonetheless, and, though perhaps awkward to use in writing and such, you can at least silently use it yourself.

In a similar way, the general semanticist Ken Keyes suggested the phrase "so far as I know." So instead of saying, "AIG is a poor insurer," you would say, "So far as I know..."

"The CEO is honest, so far as I know."

"The drug has few harmful side effects, so far as I know."

"He puts on a good conference, so far as I know."

You get the idea. We can never be sure. Keyes re-tells a funny story that makes the point:

> Plutarch tells of a Roman divorced from his wife who was blamed by his friends for the separation. "Was she not beautiful?" they asked. "Was she not chaste?"
>
> The Roman held out his shoe for them to see and asked if it were not good-looking and well-made. "Yet," he added, "none of you can tell where it pinches me."

This doesn't mean you have to go around saying "so far as I know" in front of every sentence. But Keyes suggests you feel it inside you: Your verbal maps are not complete. And you hear it, too, in the speech and writing of others – whether they say "so far as I know" or not. I find my mind automatically adding it for people when they try to assert something they can't know for sure.

Again, it's simple but effective.

Over-/Under-Defined Terms

"Begin with an individual, and before you know it you find that you have created a type; begin with a type, and you find that you have created – nothing. That is because we are all queer fish, queerer behind our faces and voices than we want any one to know or than we know ourselves."

~ F. Scott Fitzgerald, "The Rich Boy"

In his introduction to the second edition of *Science and Sanity*, Korzybski introduced a term that he said helped foster a "correct attitude toward language; namely, that most terms are 'over-/under-defined.'"

Terms are over-defined by verbal definitions taken as facts. Terms are under-defined in that they generalize about something that is only hypothetical. Most of the terms we love to use are over-/under-defined.

So, let's look at examples. Let's come up with a bunch of general nouns that I'd say fall under Korzybski's definition of over-/under-defined.

First, I'll pick some big political terms:

- Communism

- Capitalism

- Democracy

- Nation

Maybe let's throw in some financial terms:

- Profit

- Bubble

- Crash

- Cash

And some emotional terms:

- Love

- Hate

- Fear

- Greed

And some nouns that refer to things:

- Dog

- House

- Clouds

- Trees

Now, each of these terms are over-/under-defined. They each have dictionary definitions, of course. And so we can say they are over-defined "by verbal definition, because of our *belief* in the definition," as Korzybski would say. And they are hopelessly under-defined because they do not refer to anything specific in the non-verbal world. For example, "Which dog?"

Bruce Kodish writes in *Drive Yourself Sane* about a game to play with over-/under-defined words. (He credits Kenneth Johnson.) He says to create some phrase templates such as "The ___ of ___" or "___ against ___."

Now use your words to fill in the blanks. "You can end up with impressive catchphrases or book titles." I came up with "The House of Profit" and "Democracy of Fear."

You can use this as a tool for creativity, putting together words in such ways.

It's all fun and games, but Kodish reminds us that the exercise has a serious purpose: "We need to critically evaluate such higher-order abstractions by getting extentionsal. Otherwise, we can fool ourselves because our randomly formed statements can sound 'profoundly meaningful' while conveying non-sense."

This recalls the famous Sokal Affair. Alan Sokal, a physics professor at New York University, published a paper called "Transgressing the Boundaries: Towards a Transformative Hermeneutics of Quantum Gravity" in *Social Text*, an academic journal of postmodern cultural studies in the spring/summer 1996 issue.

The paper was a hoax, but the editors didn't pick up on it and published it. You can find the paper free online. I've tried to read it, but it's a slog. I can't tell you what's it about. It is full of abstractions that seem to go nowhere.

Here is how it starts:

> There are many natural scientists, and especially physicists, who continue to reject the notion that the disciplines concerned with social and cultural criticism can have anything to contribute, except perhaps peripherally, to their research. Still less are they receptive to the idea that the very foundations of their worldview must be revised or rebuilt in the light of such criticism. Rather, they cling to the dogma imposed by the long post-Enlightenment hegemony over the Western intellectual outlook, which can be summarized briefly as follows: that there exists an external world, whose properties are independent of any individual human being and indeed of humanity as a whole; that these properties are encoded in "eternal" physical laws; and that human beings can obtain reliable, albeit imperfect and tentative, knowledge of these laws by hewing to the "objective" procedures and epistemological strictures prescribed by the (so-called) scientific method.

The nonsensical article exposed the lazy thinking of the editorial staff of the journal. And it serves as a stark reminder of the danger of looking past over-/under-defined terms.

There are other stories like this. In fact, in 2014, publishers withdrew more than 120 papers from their subscription services after a French researcher discovered they were computer-generated nonsense.

Korzybski's list of over-/under-defined terms included: education, needs, intelligence, genius, teacher, leadership, sex, personality, dollar, god, gold, war, and peace, among others. A few more examples from Korzybski may help flesh out our understanding over/under-defined terms.

He canvassed professionals from a variety of fields for examples. These efforts brought back some interesting terms, such as culture and environment. Korzybski offers Mikado, which refers to the emperor of Japan. "By definition and/or creed the Mikado is supposed to be some sort of 'god.' etc. By extension or facts, the best we know, he is probably some sort of nice, supposedly educated, collegian. He has a wife and makes babies..."

We may laugh at this, but we tend to hold intensional/definitional (as opposed to extensional, or fact-based) beliefs about people with such titles as "President of the United States," "Supreme Court Judge," "Pope," or even labels such as "scientist" or "surgeon." And in finance we have "CEO" and "CFO." The analogy with "Mikado" fits neatly for these titles. By the facts, these people are something other than their vaunted definitions suggest.

If you work to bring your language down to earth, to think extensionally, as Korzybski liked to say, questions will come naturally. And you'll see many of our terms for what they are – abstractions, or made up concepts.

We always leave things out, etc.

Key Takeaways

- We can never know all the details; we always leave things out.

- Yet "all-ness" thinking is prevalent, and you can detect it in such words as *all*, *everyone*, *nobody*, *never*, *every*, and *absolutely*, among other terms.

- Korzybski recommended use of the word "etc." to remind us that we are leaving things out. ("This pencil is yellow with a nick on it, a worn down eraser and is about five inches long, etc.")

- Another tool: Robert Anton Wilson recommended the term "sombunall" to stand for "some but not all."

- And Kenneth Keyes suggested the phrase "so far as I know."

- The main idea here is for clarity of thought you should keep your language closer to the 'facts' of life, less on nebulous abstractions.

Chapter 4

Safety Devices

"[Korzybski] called quotes and hyphens "safety devices," sort of "watch out" calls to use with terms whose structural implications make them suspect."

~ Robert Pula

Korzybski advocated for the use of what he called "safety devices." These were quotation marks and hyphens. They signal a warning.

We mentioned quotation marks earlier in this book. Korzybski used single quotation marks as a way to flag a suspect term such as 'good' or 'bad.' These terms are vague labels, and a single quotation mark means we need to think about the term and be careful with it.

Single quotation marks around terms such as 'democracy' and 'value' remind us that these words are just concepts with no real existence. They are empty vessels that people fill with whatever other ideas and thoughts they want. You need to exercise care with these terms as they can quickly lead to muddled thinking.

Korzybski's convention of using single quotation marks in this way is nicely outlined in the *General Semantics Bulletin*: "to mark off terms and phrases which seem to varying degrees questionable for neurolinguistic, neurophysiological, methodological or general epistemological reasons."

You could flag nearly everything if you really wanted to be particular about it. But using single quotation marks judiciously, when you want to draw attention to a word or idea, can be helpful.

In finance, we have lots of suspect terms, such as 'stock market,' 'profits,' 'the economy,' and 'GDP.' People will use them casually, such as saying something is 'good' for the 'economy.' Good for whom exactly? And 'economy' meaning what specifically?

Sometimes people will say 'economy' and they really mean 'GDP.' So, when they say a tax cut may be 'good' for the 'economy,' what they really mean is that it will increase 'GDP.' Of course, 'GDP' is another problematic term, as we've seen. It doesn't refer to anything real. It's a vague abstraction and a term I'd put in single quotation marks.

The 'good' is an obvious problematic term. 'Good' in what way and according to whom?

Hyphens are another safety device. Hyphens bridge things that our language nudges us to think of as independent, but which the facts argue otherwise. General semanticists like to point to the terms 'mind' and 'body.' We use the terms separately, but there is no 'mind' without a 'body.' You'd think finding 'minds' was as easy as picking up sticks. You cannot separate your 'mind' from your 'body,' hence mind-body. Because of the metaphysical baggage, general semanticists often eschew the use of such problematic words as 'mind' or 'soul' altogether.

Another similar example is 'space' and 'time.' For the general semanticist, it's 'space-time.' You cannot have space that does not exist in time; and you cannot have time that exists without space. Our language fosters an illusion of separation, what Korzybski called "phantom semantic structures."

As with single quotation marks, we could link up almost every phrase we use. But used judiciously, hyphens highlight particularly harmful illusions.

General semanticists often highlight such commonplace examples as 'soul' and 'body,' 'matter' and 'spirit,' and 'thinking' and 'feeling.' General semanticists prefer, say, 'thinking-feeling.' They aim not to split verbally what cannot be split non-verbally.

Problematic Financial Terms – Almost All of Them

In finance, we have virtually endless examples of problematic terms.

The word 'earnings' is one that deserves a set of quotation marks. Conceptually, earnings are an accounting construction. They are made of estimates, and there is quite a bit of leeway in what one firm reports as 'earnings' and what another, in the same industry, reports.

This is important enough to merit a digression into accounting. For those of us engaged in security analysis, Baruch Lev and Feng Gu's *The End of Accounting* is worth a read.

The authors (both accounting professors) argue that traditional financial metrics are losing their predictive power when it comes to stock prices. They offer three big reasons:

1. The rise of intangible assets as the dominant creators of value

In the old days, physical assets tended to be the most important. Think of a factory or real estate or raw materials. But, increasingly, it's intangible assets that matter more. Think brands, know-how, patents, network effects, and the like.

Corporate investment in the latter now exceeds the former. The problem is, accounting rules treat intangibles in an odd way. As the authors point out:

> "If you develop a brand, like Coke did, it's not an asset by GAAP [generally accepted accounting principles], but if you buy it, it will proudly be displayed on your balance sheet. ... Every aspect of the financial report is adversely affected by this dated, industrial-age treatment of intangible capital."

It means that the most valuable asset a modern firm may possess – its intangible capital – gets completely missed.

2. Accounting isn't about facts

People often have trouble with this one. Readers like to quote back to me a price-earnings ratio or return on equity figure, supposing that they can take these figures at face value. As the authors write:

> Doesn't the term accounting come from *counting*, as in counting money, inventory, or product units sold? This is, however, a myth. In fact, accounting isn't about facts anymore, but rather about managers' subjective judgment, estimates, and projections.

Management decides how much depreciation to take. Management also decides how much to set aside in reserves against potential bad debts. Management classifies expenses and makes tax decisions. There is a long list of items. So you can have two companies in the same industry show very different results based on these arbitrary decisions.

One example in the book compares Boeing and Lockheed Martin. These are broadly similar firms. And yet, Boeing's return on assets (ROA) was 4.6%, compared to Lockheed's 7.1%. Big difference. Why?

Boeing and Lockheed follow different research and development strategies. Boeing develops most of its technology in-house and expenses it. Lockheed mostly acquires it and doesn't expense it. The result is that Lockheed's expenses look lower. But, as the authors write, "Is Boeing's *real* profitability so much lower than Lockheed's? Highly unlikely."

3. Unrecorded events increasingly affect corporate value

Accounting records monetary transactions. But more and more, other events drive corporate value, such as:

- Success (or failure) of drug trials
- New competitor products
- Strategic moves
- New contracts (or cancellations)
- New regulations

These events don't show up in the accounting records, at least not right away – and maybe not ever.

What to Do?

As Martin Whitman, founder of Third Avenue Value (an investment management firm based in New York), likes to say: Focus "on *what the numbers mean* rather than *what the numbers are*." (This is a message that dovetails entirely with the central project of this book.)

This is why I recommend you rarely use the accounting figures as published by the firms themselves or on websites, etc. Don't take them at face value. Spend a lot of time getting behind the numbers and getting at the real underlying economics.

Part of the authors' advice is "Forget the bottom line." There is no magic number. Analyzing a business – a complex network of people and assets subject to competition and always changing – requires you to go beyond the simple numbers.

The use of quotation marks and hyphens will help flag areas that need attention and care.

Horowitz, as always, writes eloquently on these points. On quotation marks and hyphens, he writes:

> These devices remind us, whether we like it or not, that things, beings, selves, etc. do not 'exist inherently'; they are 'empty' of 'inherent existence'... That is, there is no thing, or being, or self – no process – which exists prior to its relations with other processes that have been and are now going on outside and inside its boundaries.

We'll talk more about these points in the last section.

Key Takeaways

- Korzybski recommended the use of what he called "safety devices" to flag suspect terms.

  o Hyphens bind terms to remind us they are not separate realities (such as thinking-feeling).

  o Single quotation marks flag problematic terms such as 'good' or 'bad' – 'good' or 'bad' in what way and according to whom?

- Problematic financial terms include almost all of them. For example, 'earnings' depends a great deal on context (the accounting choices firms make, etc.)

- We looked at why traditional financial metrics may be losing their predictive power.

- Baruch Lev and Feng Gu's *The End of Accounting* advances three reasons why this may be so:

  o The rise of intangible assets as the dominant creators of value.

  o Accounting isn't about facts (it's about estimates).

  o Unrecorded events increasingly affect corporate value.

- As Martin Whitman, founder of Third Avenue Value, likes to say: Focus "*on what the numbers mean* rather than *what the numbers are.*"

Chapter 5

E-Prime

"The little word 'to be' appears as a very peculiar word and is, perhaps, responsible for many human semantic difficulties."

~ Alfred Korzybski

"You don't need to take drugs to hallucinate; improper language can fill your world with phantoms and spooks of many kinds."

~ Robert Anton Wilson

It never ceases to amaze me how many arguments the word "is" starts.

"Gold *is* money," I heard a colleague say. He expressed a popular position among devotees of the yellow metal.

"No gold *is* not money," countered another. "You can't go to the grocery store and buy anything with it."

"Gold *is* a commodity," said yet a third, "with a monetary heritage."

The conversation continued, a long and pointless argument about what gold "is." What *is* it really? We will see there is no way to answer this question in any final way without some arbitrary appeal to authority or mutual agreement.

We call this use of the word "is" the "is of identity" because it links two nouns as if they were identical, e.g., gold = money. Such arguments also persist in the realm of cryptocurrencies. For example, I've read numerous pieces where people make the case that bitcoin is or is not money. Lots of pointless debate over a definition!

Here are a few of other examples of the "is of identify" is at work:

- Bill is a value investor.
- Apple is a hardware company.
- A stock is a stock.

But as we learned earlier, these descriptions run false to facts. We know words are not the thing. The map is not the territory.

Thus, when we say gold is money, we must understand that "money" is just a word and it means different things to different people. It is not inherent in the physical characteristics of gold that it is "money." "Money" is a label people put on something, but the use of the word "is" implies somehow that gold cannot be other things, or that somehow you've said all there is to say with some finality.

The same principle is at work with these other examples. "Value investor" and "hardware company" are just definitional handles. They mean different things to different people. There is nothing inherent in either Bill or Apple that makes them those things. Nor do the labels encompass the total identities of Bill or Apple. The non-verbal person we call Bill is not the phrase "value investor." And in the phrase "a stock is a stock," we know all stocks are different from each other, yet the phrase equates them.

We will talk about ways to improve our expressions, to make them closer to the facts, in this section.

Before we do, let's look at another problematic use of "is" we call the "is of predication" (or the "is of projection") because it takes a noun and modifies it while making the modifier seem as if it is inherent to the noun.

- Apple is a cheap stock.
- That news is important.
- Eric is impatient.

In general semantics, we flag the use of "is" in this manner because we say the descriptions appear false-to-facts. The use of the word "is" acts like a sticker here. "Apple is a cheap stock" makes it sound as if on some objective level, "cheapness" is an attribute of the stock.

This is why Korzybski liked to say "whatever you say something 'is,' it is not, because that 'something' *is not* words."

To improve these phrases, we can look to eliminate the word is. On the next page, you'll see the original phrase and then an improvement:

- Bill is a value investor.
- Bill practices value investing in the style of Graham & Dodd.
- Apple is a hardware company.
- Apple generates most of its revenue from the sale of hardware.

- A stock is a stock.
- A stock seems like a stock to me.

- Apple is a cheap stock.
- Apple appears cheap at $140 per share based on its price-earnings ratio.

- That news is important.
- That news seems important to me.

- Eric is impatient.
- Eric behaves impatiently if you ask him questions he's already answered.

Of course, you could improve these statements in other ways than the ways I've shown. An easy shortcut is simply to add "to me" to everything. Or replace "is" with "seems." I'm just giving you the flavor of what you might say.

(Even expressions of color – such as "the rose is red" – are not technically accurate. As Aleister Crowley wrote in *The Book of Lies*: "A red rose absorbs all colors but red; red is therefore the one color that it is not." Even if you think that a bit much, you would still improve the description if you simply said "the rose seems red to me." After all, others may see a different color.)

Interesting things happen when you start to think this way. You start to apply these principles to what other people say. For example, an analyst of mine once said, "China is objectively a currency manipulator."

In my mind, I flagged the "is" here. In this case, he was making an argument. Stating it this way made it seem factual. It was as if he was afraid to say, "I think China manipulates its currency" because doing so leaves room for doubt. This improved version makes it clear he's expressing an opinion.

And thinking this way also helps you see clearly where the crux of an argument may lie. In this case, the magic word is "manipulates." Before even attempting to agree or disagree, my first follow-up would be: "What do you mean by manipulates?"

This technique has wide application: "This is a good business." Follow-up: "What do you mean by 'good business'?" Or: "Pfizer is over-priced." Follow-up: "What do you mean when you say 'overpriced'?"

Or we'll say something like, "Auto manufacturing is a bad business." And we say that because the industry as a whole has been a poor allocator of capital for a long time. Who can forget Fiat Chrysler's CEO Sergio Marchionne's presentation "Confessions of a Capital Junkie"? Marchionne showed the industry didn't earn its cost of capital, which means it destroyed shareholder value.

So, we might grant that "Auto manufacturing is a bad business" reflects an empirical reality. But "auto manufacturing" is a generalization. Which auto manufacturers? What are you referring to?

Because what we said about "auto manufacturing" doesn't apply to Ferrari, for example – a business that earns well in excess of its cost of capital and that, as of this writing, has been a wonderful stock since its IPO.

Anytime you see the word "is" you can mentally make a note of it as something to question. As Robert Anton Wilson put it, "any sentence containing the innocent-looking 'is' also contains a hidden fallacy."

So far, we've only looked at the word "is," but the principle works the same way for all the "to be" verbs – *be, been, were, was, am, are, is.*

A Solution to the Troublesome "To Be"

As a result, the usefulness of this exercise led some general semanticists to advocate dropping the use of "to be" verbs entirely. David Bourland Jr., who came up with the idea, called the use of the English language without the verb "*to be*" E-Prime.

Bourland had been intimately involved in general semantics and the Institute. In 1949-1950 he held a fellowship at the Institute, and later edited the General Semantics Bulletin for a time and eventually acted as a trustee.

As Bourland tells the story, in 1949 while on fellowship at the Institute he saw a letter from a man who made the suggestion to drop the verb "to be" entirely. He decided to take up the challenge and rewrote a paper he was working without using the verb "to be."

He liked the results and decided to write all his major papers that way henceforth. He didn't tell anyone about it until 1965. He coined the term "E-Prime" in an essay titled "A Linguistic Note: Writing in E-Prime."

Bourland viewed E-Prime as an additional tool to work alongside already accepted devices such as the indexes, dates, quotes, hyphens, etc. that we've been discussing in Part II.

The short six-page essay makes some striking points. First, it includes a wonderful quote from the philosopher George Santayana:

> The little word *is* has its tragedies; it names and identifies different things with the greatest innocence; and yet no two are ever identical, and if therein lies the charm of wedding them and calling them one, therein too lies the danger. Whenever I use the word *is*, except in sheer tautology, I deeply misuse it; and when I discover my error, the world seems to fall asunder, and the members of my family no longer know one another.

So you see this isn't the sole province of cranky linguists and general semanticists. It's been something that thoughtful people from a range of disciples and times have pondered, including such famous thinkers as Thomas Hobbes, Bertrand Russell, and Alfred North Whitehead.

Bourland includes another quote, even older, from Augustus de Morgan, a British mathematician. I include part of it here:

> The most difficult inquiry which anyone can propose to himself is to find out what any thing *is*: in all probability we do not know what we are talking about when we ask such a question.

This sounds like something right of out Korzybski. E-Prime, then, has something of a rich, if hidden, history.

But what effect does it really have? What benefits could one enjoy by using E-Prime?

Well, it has a way of making questions vanish. There are some questions you cannot ask in E-Prime. (For example: "What is gold?") Bourland would argue that any question structured with an "is" takes you down a path of discourse where you severely reduce the odds of exchanging useful information. Put another way, avoiding "is" gets you out of the dead end of arguing about definitions and instead focuses how things work, behave, etc. (To recast the gold question, you might ask: "How does gold behave?")

Another point Bourland makes is the verb "to be" encourages, or forces, abbreviation. Instead of describing how Bill invests, you just slap a sticker on him. "Bill is a value investor." Instead of being more considered in your judgment about Eric's impatient behavior, the verb "to be" gives you the easy way out: "Eric is impatient." Instead of focusing on China's specific actions with regard to its currency, you can skate out of it by just declaring, "China is a currency manipulator."

Bourland uses this example: "We do this thing because it is right." You could write volumes about those last three words, and certainly people have. There are libraries of books trying to figure out what "is" right. Bourland writes:

> One may find it an interesting exercise to recast that statement in E-Prime, while preserving the presumed intent of the original statement. I suggest this as one possibility: "We do this thing because we sincerely desire to minimize the discrepancies between our actions and our stated 'ideals'." That form obviously does not have the pithy snap of the original statement. Some would probably characterize that particular E-Prime variant as somewhat pedestrian. Even so, the E-Prime statement seems to admit openly the participation in the overall situation of some creed or set of beliefs, allegedly held currently by some humans and subject to change (although perhaps only after some considerable struggle.)

With E-Prime, you will find it more difficult to make snappy generalizations. You will find it harder to pass off abstractions as some kind of 'fact.' E-Prime exposes beliefs from hiding.]

Third, Bourland says E-Prime brings out the role players. Without E-Prime you can smuggle in unidentified opinions. "The stock is cheap." Says who? "It is right." Again, says who? E-Prime forces you to bring out the agents involved. ("The stock seems cheap to Robert.")

Enthusiasts of E-Prime tend to overstate their case. In the anthology, *To Be or Not: An E-Prime Anthology*, you'll find the case for speaking in E-Prime, along with a weak attempt at fiction in E-Prime and even the re-working of aphorisms into E-Prime. For example, Ralph Waldo Emerson said: "There is properly no history, only biography." Reworked in E-Prime, you might render it this way: "History does not exist, only interlocking biographies." (Demerits for E-Prime's literary elegance.)

And if you haven't had enough, there is a second and a third E-Prime anthology with more of the same – a piling on of examples and advocacy. But enough is enough at some point. For me, I like E-Prime as a tool. I like what it teaches. I even tried my hand at writing a few essays in E-Prime. (No one noticed, which I take as a good thing. It means you can do it and it does not have to be awkward.) Robert Anton Wilson was another big proponent of E-Prime. He wrote a whole book in E-Prime. (*Quantum Psychology*. I recommend it.)

Nonetheless, I do not plan to write or speak in E-Prime and nor do I recommend you do so. The verb "to be" serves other functions that would be lost with E-Prime. Moreover, many of the uses of "to be" seem innocuous and not worth fussing over. (And there is the matter of literary elegance mentioned previously.) Besides, you can still commit all kinds of semantic 'fouls' in E-Prime. I think it enough to get the idea of E-Prime and use it as a tool in your critical and analytical framework. There's no reason to get dogmatic about it.

English Minus Absolutes

E-Prime is somewhat controversial in general semantic circles. James D. French, a computer programmer at the University of California, Berkeley, wrote a good summary of some arguments against using it in a paper titled "The Top Ten Arguments Against E-Prime." The paper is succinct and easy to read. I won't rehash it here, but I'll share his No. 1 argument against E-Prime, which is a powerful one:

> E-Prime makes no distinction between statements that cross the principles of general semantics and statements that do not. A statement such as, "I am going to the store," violates no formulation of general semantics, yet E-Prime prohibits it.

In some ways, E-Prime's prohibitions against all forms of the verb "to be" remind me of another prohibition. It is like saying having too much alcohol is bad, so let's ban alcohol entirely. I prefer to retain the richness of the language and instead use E-Prime as a probe to detect potential hidden fallacies, errors of logic, etc.

Allen Walker Read (1906-2002), another prominent general semanticist, didn't favor E-Prime, but argued for what he called "English Minus Absolutisms" in a paper titled "Language Revision by Deletion of Absolutisms."

The idea here is simple enough. Reflect on our four basic tenets that opened Part II. They draw you to a conclusion: our knowledge is imperfect and often probabilistic. Therefore, we should avoid using absolutistic terms. As Read puts it: "Can we ever find 'perfection' or 'certainty' or 'truth'? No! Then let us stop using such words in our formulations."

Absolutisms include words such as "always," "never," "certain," "perfect," "intolerable," "ineradicable," "insoluble," "incorrigible," "interminable," "impregnable," "infallible," etc.

"Foremost among the words to be eliminated is the word certain," Read writes. "It is very easy to begin a sentence with, "I'm certain that ... "; but it is just as easy to say, "It seems to me that ..."

I think he makes a good point. It's not hard to do. But again, it's not that I won't ever use those words again. I can imagine plenty of situations where they're harmless. (On the golf course: "Dang, that drive was perfect!" Well, it was not literally *perfect*, but who really cares...)

But as an investor, if you hear absolutist phrases, you might want to train your mind to linger on them a moment and ask: "Is that really so?" Because it won't be. And perhaps therein lies an interesting line of questioning.

As Keyes says, most of the time, our "maps" will be more accurate if we say:

- "Many" instead of "all"
- "Usually" instead of "always"
- "Seldom" instead of "never"
- "Similar" instead of "same"
- Etc.

How Do You Know?

In the end, E-Prime and English Minus Absolutisms, along with the other tools in Part II, are only useful in sensible hands.

I'll give the last word to Robert Pula, who always seems so wise and reasonable on so many matters: "No technique is guaranteed to free us from the responsibility of our own evaluatings. Even applications of the extensional devices [dates, indexing, etc.] seem destined not to 'save' use if we don't pay sufficient attention to what we're doing *while we're doing it*."

Key Takeaways

- We looked at the potentially troublesome nature of the word "is" and how its use can smuggle in a hidden fallacy.

- For example, the use of the word "is" can act like a sticker. Saying "Apple is a cheap stock" makes it sound as if on some objective level, "cheapness" is an attribute of the stock. Better would be to say "Apple seems cheap..."

- The principle works the same for all the "to be" verbs – *be, been, were, was, am, are, is.*

- This led to the creation of E-Prime – English without using the verb "to be."

- Another variation is "English Minus Absolutisms" advocated by Allen Walker Read (1906-2002), another prominent general semanticist. EMA is English without words such as never, always, perfect, best, etc.

- Our maps are more accurate when we use language that reflects more carefully the nuance of the world out there. (Use "seldom" instead of "never," "many" instead of "all," etc.)

Chapter 6

Either/Or Logic – Add a Maybe

"Mankind likes to think in terms of extreme opposites. It is given to formulating beliefs in terms of *Either-Ors*, between which it recognizes no intermediate possibilities."

~ John Dewey (1859-1952), philosopher

"There two kinds of people in this world: those who always divide the people of the world into two kinds, and those who don't."

~ Anonymous

Maurice Hindus, a prolific author on Soviet and Central European affairs, once interviewed a Soviet professor of philosophy in the 1960s. Here is an account of part of the exchange:

> "Einstein," [Hindus] said, "was one of the greatest scientists of all time, and so far as I know he never accepted the philosophy of dialectical materialism."
>
> "We have translated the book Einstein wrote with Enfield [Infeld]. We study the book because the authors are great scientists. But we reject their idealistic doctrines."
>
> "Suppose the student sees the merits of these doctrines?"
>
> "We argue him out of it."
>
> "But suppose he remains unconvinced?"
>
> "Impossible. We have the question period and we hold seminars and in the end we defeat our ideological enemies."
>
> "But if the student persists in contradicting the professor?"
>
> "It doesn't happen. It cannot happen. Our arguments are incontrovertible."

"And if it were to happen?"

This time the professor replied solemnly: "Then the student would be place himself outside of our Soviet society."

S.I. Hayakawa, who taught general semantics (and eventually went on to become a U.S. senator) cited this interview in his book *Language in Thought and Action* as an example of Either/Or thinking. Either you agreed with Marxism or you were an outcast. That is the nature of Either/Or thinking. It admits no gradation or matters of degree. It's only good/bad, true/false, hot/cold, etc.

The Soviet professor may sound quaint, or may sound like a relic of something we don't have to worry about anymore, but Either/Or thinking is alive and well.

George W. Bush famously said, "You're either with us or against us in the fight against terror." Either/Or thinking. There is no middle ground. He's not the first or last person to invoke the "you're either with us or against" routine.

I remember a conversation with friends where one criticized Obama for something and another friend of mine right away started talking about how Bush did X and Y. The implication being that the Obama critic was a Bush supporter. Again, Either/Or. You're either an Obama supporter (Democrat) or you must be a Republican.

Politics is a place where it's easy to see Either/Or thinking. But it's really everywhere. A neat little exercise I recommend is to read the paper (or wherever you get your news) and look for examples of Either/Or thinking. You'll find plenty of examples.

I have a financial example from a conversation I had recently with a friend. We were talking about how pervasive passive investing has become and what effects it might have on basic price discovery. (Passive investing means investing in ETFs or indexes, where no human being is directly making buy/sell decisions in the fund. Instead, the fund follows a pre-determined model portfolio. Passive investing stands in contrast to active investing, where human beings decide what to buy/sell.)

My friend argued that you needed very little active management to keep a functioning market with price discovery. He threw out the number 2%, citing experiments by MIT finance professor Andrew Lo. In other words, you only need 2% of the market to be actively managed (by people, trying to figure out what things are worth) and the rest could be on autopilot (in index ETFs, for example) and you wouldn't impede price discovery.

Underlying this argument, of course, is the idea that the market functions or it doesn't, that there is price discovery or there isn't. Instead, doesn't it seem more likely that there are gradations at work here? Maybe parts of the market function well and parts don't.

And besides, what's so magical about 2%? So at 1.9% we're no good and 2.1% we're okay? By this point, using the tools in this book, you can come up lots of questions and objections with Lo's 2% argument – and you don't even need a PhD in finance.

What general semantics encourages is a multi-valued logic. As Weinberg puts it, "How bad, how good, what degree of guilt, how dark, what shade of gray, how much more for me, how much against me?"

It is convenient to classify things as either/or, but such 'maps' run false to facts.

Even labeling something as poisonous or not poisonous is not quite true to facts. "There is nothing so poisonous that a small amount can be taken without harm," Keyes reminds us in his sensible little book *How to Develop Your Thinking Ability*, "and there is nothing so nonpoisonous that a huge amount can be imbued safely... Anything can be poisonous if you absorb enough; nothing is poisonous if you take a sufficiently small quantity."

As he points out, torture chambers in the Middle Ages found that large quantities of water forced into a human stomach was quite an effective poison.

Thus, several 20th-century scientists came up with multi-valued logics to replace the Aristotelian either/or. (Though, this isn't necessarily about replacing one with the other. We can use both and there are applications for which only an either/or orientation will do.)

Going Beyond Either/Or

"All statements are true in some sense, false in some sense, meaningless in some sense, true and false in some sense, true and meaningless in some sense, false and meaningless in some sense, and true and false and meaningless in some sense."

~ Greg Hill, *Principia Discordia*

Some ways to go beyond Either/Or are simple, such as three-valued logic: "yes," "no" and "maybe." The latter is one of my favorite words.

Keyes liked using "up to a point" as a qualifier to introduce the matter of degrees or gradations. So consider these questions:

- Is he a better investor than I am?
- Am I a better investor than him?
- Are politicians honest?
- Are CEOs honest?
- Is this a good business?
- Is this a cheap stock?

To answer each, you could use "up to a point." For each answer may be true some of the time or in certain circumstances. (And putting aside, for the moment, problematic terms such as 'honest,' 'good,' 'cheap,' etc.) "Up to a point" is like a "maybe" and many other like phrases – such as "possibly," "to a degree," "to some extent," etc. – that open up a third way, beyond Either/Or logic.

Then there is Anatol Rapoport's four-valued logic, "true, false, indeterminate and meaningless." Remember the logic of Irving Lee's fact versus inference (discussed earlier)? We assert some things as having a high probability (as near to certain as human beings can be) of being 'true' or 'false.' Rapoport adds "indeterminate" and "meaningless."

The author Robert Anton Wilson explains this well in *Quantum Psychology*. Meaningless means, "we cannot, even in theory, imagine a way of testing it."

One example he gives is: "All living beings contain souls which cannot be seen or measured." He contrasts this with the statement: "Water boils at 45 degrees Fahrenheit at sea level on this planet." The latter lends itself to testing and refutation, the former does not.

How Do You Know?

In the financial world, I've come up with several meaningless statements:

- Risk-taking is the soul of capitalism.

- Gold is real money.

- Humility is the key to being a great investor.

To answer the first we'd have to go out and find the 'soul of capitalism' and get it in a lab. Even then, 'risk-taking' is one of those words that need clarification. For gold, there is no way to know what 'real money' is, as we discussed. 'Money' is a concept; people make it up. The last statement about humility is also untestable and is a variant of what you've probably seen all over the place. It's mere assertion.

Indeterminate means something that is at least theoretically testable, but not at present. They are far more troublesome in the financial world than meaningless statements. Some examples:

- Macy's stock has hit bottom.

- Jeff Bezos is the best CEO in America.

- Coca-Cola has a durable competitive advantage.

To answer the first, we need time. We can only tell if Macy's has hit bottom in retrospect. There is no way to know whether this statement is true today. As for Jeff Bezos, we could imagine a test of some sort, but it would be rather arbitrary. Other people might come up with a different test and get a different result. For Coca-Cola, we can speculate about its competitive advantage (however we choose to define what that means), but it's not knowable now how durable it is. Only time will tell.

An easy way to keep the ideas of "meaningless" and "indeterminate" apart:

- Meaningless means forever untestable.

- Indeterminate means not yet testable.

Sorting out statements this way will save you some time and brainpower. It's also another tool to get you beyond "Either/Or." Next time someone asks you if X statement is true or false, you can add that it is perhaps meaningless or indeterminate.

Though I will not get into it here, Lotfi Zadeh's fuzzy logic is an approach that has similarities to general semantics. (See "Fuzzy Logic and General-Semantics in Everyday Life" by Susan Presby Kodish, Ph.D., and Bruce I. Kodish.) Fuzzy logic, among other things, embraces a non-Aristotelian orientation that goes beyond either/or categories. It embraces degrees, shades of gray, etc.

As author Bruce Kodish writes in *Drive Yourself Sane*:

> Fuzzy logic can be used to formulate in a mathematically exact manner how something can be considered both A and not-A. It has been successfully applied, especially by the Japanese, in designing machine control systems.

Fuzzy logic sounds daunting, but a simple example may help. Let us say I ask you: "Do you like where you live?" It is conceivable you both like and dislike where you live. There are aspects of it you like and aspects you don't like. Fuzzy logic is a sophisticated, mathematical approach dealing with the concept of partial truth, or degrees of truth.

Lastly, a subtext to this either/or discussion is that, as Robert Anton Wilson liked to emphasize, reality is always plural. There is no 'ultimate reality.' There is only a 'reality' as measured by a certain instrument at a certain time and certain place, whether that instrument is our nervous system or something like a thermometer. A thermometer measures only heat; it says nothing about length. It is not "more accurate" than a yardstick. The two instruments reflect different realities.

All of these aforementioned ideas ought to propel you beyond the pitfalls of Either/Or thinking.

Key Takeaways

- We looked at the problems with either/or thinking – right or wrong, good or bad, success or failure, etc.

- We instead advocated for a multi-valued logic where we grade things on a scale.

- We also introduced Anatole Rapoport's 4-valued logic: "true, false, indeterminate and meaningless."

- Reality is always plural. There isn't one reality.

How Do You Know?

Chapter 7

IFD Disease and the Happiness Formula

"We may call it IFD disease: from idealism to frustration to demoralization. Probably no one of us entirely escapes it. It is of epidemic proportions… a condition out of which there tend to develop the various types of severe 'mental' and nervous disorders…"

~ Wendell Johnson, *People in Quandaries*

Wendell Johnson (1906-1965), among other things, wrote one of the better popularizations of general semantics, called *People in Quandaries* (1946). As a psychologist and speech therapist, his book mostly deals with general semantics as psychotherapy.

In studying what makes people unhappy and miserable, he found similarities in how they adjusted to, and thought about, events and the world around them. The chief villain on equanimity seems to be our ideals, or the ideals 'society' hands to us. These ideals prove elusive. Unable to achieve the ideals, we feel frustration.

Johnson's contention was that our language encouraged frustration because of how easily it lapses into either/or thinking. For example, we tend to label things as 'success' or 'failure.' There isn't an easy word for something that lies between. There is 'bigger' and there is 'better.' There isn't usually room for 'good enough.'

In other words, people who were unhappy and frustrated tended to be those who accepted unrealistically high standards, as encouraged by our Aristotelian language. Johnson wrote:

> Quandaries, then, are rather like verbal cocoons in which individuals elaborately encase themselves, and from which, under circumstance common in our time, they do not tend to hatch. The peculiar structure of these cocoons appears to be determined in great measure by the structure of the society in which they are formed – and the structure of this society has been and continues to be determined significantly by the structure of the language which we so unconsciously acquire and so unreflectively employ. Simply by using bad language and by living in terms of the basic orientation which it represents and fosters, we tend to

cultivate the idealism and so to suffer the frustration and demoralization which are so conspicuous in the lives of people in quandaries.

Verbal cocoons! What a great phrase for what we do to ourselves. In essence it points the finger at language as the culprit – or one culprit – behind unhappiness. More specifically, our use of absolutist language fosters discontent.

For example, "I want to be a successful investor," is vague. Phrased that way, you may never meet that goal and seed IFD disease. It is akin to saying "I want to be happy." What is 'happy'? IFD encourages you to be specific and shed absolutes and also question the ideals handed to you by 'society.'

'Society's' ideals can impoverish your life if you let them. These ideals create never-ending wants to be better-looking, smarter, richer, healthier, happier, etc. Wear these clothes. Go to this school. Learn this trade. Eat these foods. Think these thoughts. Etc. The wheel of 'progress' never ends – everything has got to be faster, bigger, better, etc.

At some point, you have to wonder what it's all for? What good does it do? Is it worth the anxious neurotic personalities it seems to produce in great numbers? If it's all a bunch of abstractions anyway, what difference does it all make?

Ah, the latter is a big question and we'll get to this in the last chapter...

For now, let's circle back on IFD disease. Korzybski himself had formulated an "extensional theory of happiness," which surely inspired Johnson to come up with IFD. Korzybski's idea basically was to not expect too much, to keep your expectations low. (Though this did not mean you couldn't have goals and work toward them.) If you did this, you would not get bitter or cynical when "bumping against the facts" in actual life.

In investing, you can apply this idea readily by tamping down your expectations for your own performance. To set out to make 20% every year is a recipe for IFD disease. The life-facts of investing show it is an uneven ride through peaks and valleys, even for the very best of our profession.

Consider the famous study by Eugene Shahan in 1986. In that study, Shahan looked at a number of great investors.

You can see them ranked by their total annual return and the number of years they did it (as of the 1986 study):

Manager	Total Annual Return (%)	No. of Years
Warren Buffett	23.8	13
Pacific Partners	23.6	19
Stan Perlmeter	19.0	18
Sequoia Fund	18.2	13 3/4
Walter Schloss	16.1	28 1/4
Tweedy, Browne	16.0	15 3/4
Charles Munger	13.7	14

Those are numbers that any investor would be delighted to achieve. And yet, these investors underperformed the market averages about a third of the time. Pacific Partners had six years in a row in which they trailed the market. And yet their numbers are just a shade below Buffett's.

Then there is John Templeton (1912-2008). *Templeton's Way with Money: Strategies and Philosophy of a Legendary Investor* by Jonathan Davis and Alasdair Nairn covers his investment career better than any other book I've come across.

A bit of background on Templeton: He started the Templeton Growth Fund in 1954. This would be his flagship fund. He ran it until 1992. The average return was about 16% per year for 38 years.

This was almost four points better than the market over that time, an astonishing record. He did it without using debt and often had excess cash. If you had put $10,000 with Templeton in 1954 and left it there, you had $1.7 million when he stepped down in 1992. That's a 170-fold return.

However, he wasn't good all the time. His fund lost money in 10 of those 38 years – almost 25% of the time. From 1971 to 1975, he trailed the market in three years out of five. Every time he did, the media would come out and write stories about how he lost his touch. Incredibly, for the first 10 years of the fund's life, Templeton trailed the MSCI World Index. Today's impatient investors would likely fire such a manager.

This reminds me of an example from Nassim Taleb's book *Fooled by Randomness*. He imagines an exceptional investor who earns 15% per year with volatility of 10% per year. Statistically, this means his chance of earning money in any given year is 93%. (I'll spare you the math).

Over shorter time intervals, though, odds of success drop a bunch, as Taleb showed:

Time frame	Probability of making money
1 year	93%
1 quarter	77%
1 month	67%
1 day	54%

The point is that over short periods of time there is a lot of noise. Even with the odds greatly tipped in your favor, there is a fair chance you can still lose money over short time frames. And it's a cinch you'll see poor results for perhaps a third of the time even on an annual basis.

Investment results are, by their nature, uneven and fickle. Superior results come not by trying to beat the market all the time, but by trying to find ways to tilt the odds in your favor and then by being patient.

Empathy – And the Rise and Fall of Bill Miller

Bill Miller managed the Legg Mason Value Fund, and he beat the S&P 500 for 15 years straight – from 1991 to 2005. He became much celebrated as a result.

Janet Lowe wrote a fawning book about him called *The Man Who Beats the S&P: Investing With Bill Miller*. It came out in 2002. Lowe probed Miller's thinking. She called him the "go-to guy for new economy value investing." Miller as portrayed here was a brainy guy with wide-ranging interests, who went to the Santa Fe Institute, read about physics, complexity, chaos theory and more. He pondered "buttons and thread, ant colonies and even alluvial geography."

Bill Miller himself was more circumspect about his market-beating run. In his fourth-quarter 2005 letter he wrote:

> You are probably aware that the Legg Mason Value Trust has outperformed the S&P 500 index for each of the past 15 calendar years. This may be the reason you decided to purchase the fund. If so, we are flattered, but believe you are setting yourself up for disappointment. While we are pleased to have performed as we have, our so-called

"streak" is a fortunate accident of the calendar. Over the past 15 years, the December-to-December time frame is the only one of the 12-month periods where our results have always outpaced those of the index.

He was right. The glory years wouldn't last. In December 2008, *The Wall Street Journal* ran a long story by Tom Lauricella titled "The Stock Picker's Defeat." Miller no longer resided at the top of the profession, but found himself at the bottom, crushed under the weight of a 58% loss in the value of his fund. It wiped away years of outperformance and dropped him among the worst performers for the previous one-, three-, five-, and 10-year periods.

"Why didn't I just throw my money out of the window – and light it on fire?" one investor asked. There were rumors Miller would be replaced. His style, so celebrated while he was on top, was now seen as almost foolish, pig-headed, risky, broken…

I have a copy of that *Wall Street Journal* story, which I keep tucked in my copy of Lowe's book. It serves as a reminder that 'success' in our business is fragile. It reminds me that good performance, even over a long period of time, can dissolve quickly.

And this brings me to the idea of empathy.

Definitions go against the thrust of this book, but we can describe empathy by how we feel: You feel empathy toward another person when you think of what it might be like to be in their shoes, as the saying goes. It is when you experience their feelings and emotions vicariously.

Gad Horowitz in *Radical General Semantics* describes empathy also by comparing it to what it is not: when we blame, demonize, condemn, in absolutist, moral terms another human being, we can say we are not feeling empathetic.

Horowitz recommends a new device, one to use alongside such other devices we've learned about to this point: indexing, dating, quotation marks, etc. The point of this new device would be to trigger feelings of empathy. You would attach an "EM" to an individual's name, like this: Bill Miller EM.

Seeing the "EM" would trigger the realization that "if instead of Bill Miller, it had been me who was conceived in the womb of Bill's mother, with exactly the same genetic materials and at exactly the same moment, and then lived through

---

How Do You Know?

the very same prenatal and postnatal experiences, and in the same sequence, well then, I would have been Bill Miller." (Horowitz doesn't use Bill Miller as an example. He uses Adolf Hitler, which has greater shock value, but perhaps to a distracting degree.)

"In my opinion," Horowitz writes, "it would be excessively rigorous simply to dismiss this as a tautology. Read it again and you may see that it is actually a necessary implication of the chain-index." (You may recall our discussion of the chain index earlier.)

The EM device – which Horowitz says is "a secularized version of the Christian aphorism there but for the grace of God go I" – reminds us that much is not in our control. We are products of a process we don't fully understand.

If general semantics is partially about clear thinking, about creating maps more accurate for the territory they represent, then the EM device serves a useful purpose. As with these other devices, I encourage you to work with them. After a time, they become second nature to you and you won't even need to actually put an "EM" after a person's name. You'll do it automatically, silently.

As Horowitz points out, you can use it on yourself. Self-empathy.

Key Takeaways

- We introduced Wendell Johnson's IFD Disease: from idealism to frustration to demoralization.

- Our language encourages frustration because we think in terms of ideals and absolutes.

- To avoid IFD Disease, you have to tamp down your expectations.

- We looked at Eugene Shahan's famous study, which showed how even great investors deliver years of sub-par performance in the midst of their careers.

- Great investors are not great all the time.

- We looked at the rise and fall of Legg Mason's Bill Miller and introduced another device: "EM," standing for empathy. EM reminds you of the shifting winds of fortune, of which none of us are immune, and perhaps you will judge more gently your fellow human beings.

Chapter 8

The Delayed Reaction

"One of the aims of general semantics training is the development of the habit of delaying responses, thus increasing the chances that our responses will be more appropriate for the situation."

~ Harry Weinberg, general semanticist, *Levels of Knowing and Existence*

"Reserving judgments is a matter of infinite hope."

~ F. Scott Fitzgerald, *The Great Gatsby*

This short section serves as a sort of coda for Part II. In a sense, all the devices (indexing, dating, etc.) discussed in Part II are ways to get you to slow down and think more about what you are saying or thinking, or what others are saying to you.

Korzybski put it this way:

> The stress on delayed reactions is not new "wisdom." There is an age-old saying, 'When mad count to ten.' Practically all human maladjustments, including most neuroses and psychoses, involved undelayed reactions; hence the *preventative* and even therapeutic value of the introduction of permanent automatic delayed reactions, for a fraction of a second, which prevents 'emotional' outbursts.

Try to delay your assessments. This is hard to do in a Twitter-feed world, but the wisdom of delayed reactions can manifest itself in so many different ways.

I was at a conference once early in my career as an investment writer. After I spoke, a guy dressed in overalls – yes, overalls – walked up to me and asked me a question I've long forgotten. But what I remember first is how I judged this person when he came up to me: Overalls, somewhat shabby in appearance, with a bushy beard… must be some sort of country bumpkin. Gosh, I hope this conversation is brief.

However, after talking to him, I found out he was a very wealthy man and a smart investor, too. I remember thinking to my young self, "I will never make an assumption like that again."

This anecdote has stuck with me to this day. And at conferences when I meet people I am careful to reserve judgment on that person for as long as I can. In this case, many men in overalls may well be country bumpkins, but that fact – if it is a fact – says nothing about the man who stood in front of me then.

As investors, delayed reactions can make you some money. I can recall times when I heard an investor share an idea on a stock whose name I know and which I think I know something about. "Let me tell you, I really like GM…" this person might begin. It is hard to fight back an immediate eye roll. "GM? Really? I know the story." But do you?

Again, I always try to wait, hear the person out. Maybe there is a wrinkle now that makes it interesting. I remember when my analyst came to me with CIT Group, a firm that went bankrupt in the financial crisis of 2008 and cost its investors a lot of money. Definitely a tarnished name…

Yet, the year was 2016. Things had changed. The company slogged through a long restructuring. This had left it with a strong balance sheet. It had just agreed to sell its aircraft leasing business. Once closed, this would leave it with a huge slug of cash, almost one-third of its market cap. Yet despite all this progress, the stock traded in the penalty box, at a big discount to other banks. It was a compelling idea. And there were no big-name investors in it. CIT Group seemed left for dead. We bought it and in less than six months we were up almost 30%.

I have also been on the other side, as I am sure you have, where you get the definite sense that someone isn't really listening to you. Once my analyst and I made a presentation on Tucows, which owns Ting Mobile along with a domain name business and an emerging fiber business. It had been a 10-bagger in the previous 5 years.

And I remember talking to someone about it afterward who seemed overly focused on the fact that Tucows had already gone up tenfold and, as a result, sort of shrugged off the idea, as if it had already played out. He seemed to know the idea but I could tell that he was not quite up to date. Needless to say, the stock more than doubled in the ensuing 12 months. Had he delayed his initial reaction, he might've listened more carefully to my thesis and bought the stock.

Let's think more about why a delayed reaction has value. It comes down to what we're reacting to. What we react to is words and symbols. But, as we know by now, these words/symbols are not the things they represent. They are abstractions. And it takes some time – sometimes fractions of a second, sometimes much longer periods of time – to connect the abstraction to the thing it represents in a reliable and accurate way.

Wendell Johnson put it well:

> This is true in part because what it represents is never two times the same. One's reaction therefore, is to be correspondingly delayed and the variable, since there is clearly a disadvantage, as a rule, in being overly ready to react in any rigidly set way.

Johnson makes the point that the methods used by Pavlov in getting dogs to salivate at the sound of bells (which the dogs learn to automatically associate with treats) is much the same method used by totalitarians such as Hitler to get people to respond to swastikas and the like with "monotonously *consistent* and *undelayed* gestures, attitudes and elaborate courses of action."

Advertising works the same way. Advertisers aim to get a reaction from slogans and symbols, to get you to act or think a certain way. The anarchist thinker and poet Peter Lamborn Wilson relates advertising to image magic. It's a way to manipulate people's thinking. And it works, or there wouldn't be so much of it.

Your defense against this begins with recognition of words and symbols as abstractions. Awareness of abstractions cultivates a tendency to delay your reactions. You'll know the word or symbol is not the thing.

Johnson again:

> This delay is essential to adequate evaluation. If all *Jews,* or all *physicians,* or all *blondes*, are not the same, then we cannot have one response to be made without hesitation to every *Jew,* or to every *physician,* or to every *blonde,* on every occasion. Then we must have various possibilities of reaction and we must delay them in any particular instance until an appropriate response becomes apparent.

If you absorb these ideas you'll look at everything in a different way. You won't read the newspaper or your favorite websites in the same way ever again. It can be done, but it takes some practice.

I have been working with these ideas and concepts for about two years. I am at the point where I see abstractions riddled through articles and research. I easily see the abstractions when people speak in advertisements, in political speech, etc. It is as if these little flags pop up in my mind. And these flags naturally prompt questions. I find it sharpens my thinking and analysis immensely. It relaxes my mind, too, in that it is much harder for other people to get me riled up than before. I simply don't react to the abstractions the way they do. I see the nonsense.

Please understand: I am not saying all abstractions are bad or that we should avoid them all. We have to use them and live with them. But we don't want to respond in a conditioned or invariable way to them and behave like Pavlov's dogs. We can learn to delay our reactions and think through the abstractions. The tools in Part II help you do that.

Key Takeaways

- Try to delay your assessments.

- It takes some time – sometimes this time may just be fractions of a second, sometimes much longer periods of time – to connect the abstraction to the thing it represents in a reliable and accurate way.

- The wisdom of delayed reactions can manifest itself in so many different ways, some of which we discuss in this chapter.

Part III
Chapel Perilous

Chapel Perilous

"In his books, and most importantly in his autobiography Cosmic Trigger, [author] Robert Anton Wilson talks about the psychological state where you have no way of making sense of what is happening, where all your maps have run out, and where you have no fixed point with which to orient yourself by. He called this place Chapel Perilous. This is where we are now…"

~ John Higgs, author

After all the ground we've covered, you may feel a little disoriented, as if there is almost no knowledge you can depend on absolutely. For every assertion, there are qualifications; for every belief, there are reasons to doubt; and for every theory, there is potential for revision, if not eventual rejection entirely.

Welcome to Chapel Perilous.

At the start of this book, we began with the idea that what we think about investing, Wall Street, and life rests on abstractions – words and symbols that do not have any real existence in the non-verbal world "out there." Yet, we treat them as if they are real. We allow them to shackle our thinking and bind our actions, almost as if by magic.

In Part I, we covered many of the ways we create abstractions and how they are different from what these abstractions aim to describe. And we looked at the many ways the world is far more complex, and our understanding of it far more limited, than we generally assume.

In Part II, we focused on practical tools to help us see through these abstractions, to remind us of their shortcomings and sharpen our thinking.

In Part III, we try to tie all this together. We'll also push out to what I think are some of the boldest conclusions we can draw from general semantics and related ideas.

And once again, forced to summarize, I'd turn to our four propositions:

1. Our world changes continuously; nothing stays the same

2. No two things exist exactly alike

3. Observer and observed create what the observer sees

4. We can never know all the details; we always leave things out

These four propositions make the case for intellectual humility if nothing else.

And so, you probably have a better understanding of my answer to the question: How do we know? The answer is we don't really know. And we can't.

Intellectual humility also applies to the book in your hands. It is a kind of 'thinking out loud.' I am reminded of what Alan Watts wrote in one of his books, "If... I sometimes make statements in an authoritative and dogmatic manner, it is for the sake of clarity rather than from the desire to pose as an oracle." The same applies here.

Watts thought it a great mistake to avoid publishing something because you were not ready to defend it to death. It goes against the spirit of play and the desire to explore ideas and to learn from criticism. You should not fear changing your mind; ergo you should not fear putting out an opinion because you might be 'wrong.'

'Truth' is a tricky thing, after all. Another thinker who understood our inability to get at 'truth' (and who Alfred Korzybski influenced) was Gregory Bateson (1904-1980). A social scientist whose work connected several fields, he explained Korzybski's map is not the territory analogy as a reminder of an ever-present gap between "the report and the thing reported, the *Ding an sich.*" (The German phrase means the thing as it is in itself, unmediated by perception and language, an essentially unknowable quality of endless detail. Think of Korzybski's pencil.)

'Truth,' then, could be thought of as a "precise correspondence between our description and what we describe," as Bateson puts it. But this is impossible, as we've shown in this book. Thus, all our knowledge is at best provisional.

H.L. Mencken (1880-1956), the great wit and author, voiced this same skepticism in a characteristically memorable way:

> I am never absolutely certain that I am right, and for the plain reason
> that I am never absolutely certain that anything is true. It may *seem* to
> me to be true and I may be quite unable to imagine its falsity – but that
> is simply saying my imagination is limited, not that the proposition itself
> is immovably sound. Some other man, better born than I was or drinking

better liquor, may disprove it tomorrow. And if not tomorrow, then day after tomorrow, or maybe next week, or next year. I know of no so-called truth that quite escapes this possibility. Anything is conceivable in a world so irrational as this one.

We can improve our theories (our maps). We can sometimes disprove them. But we can never prove anything "except in the realms of totally abstract tautology." This gap between our perception and the thing perceived forever tempers what we think we know. 'Truth,' in the sense described here, is not obtainable.

Of Korzybski's great project, Bateson wrote: "Korzybski was, on the whole, speaking as a philosopher attempting to persuade people to discipline their manner of thinking. But he could not win."

He could not win because, Bateson contended, our reactions were biological and emotional and not subject to logical discourse in many situations.

I like one of Bateson's situations, which clearly shows what he's talking about. He writes how the American flag is perceived as a symbol for the country of the United States. It is, however, not the country itself. But our brains don't draw this distinction well. When people stomp on the flag and burn it, the response you feel may well be rage. "And this rage," Bateson writes, "will not be diminished by an explanation of map-territory relations."

For many situations and for many people (perhaps most?), what Bateson says may be true. But I remain optimistic that with self-study and practice with the ideas covered in this book, you can improve your perceptions such that you more readily see through abstractions than before (and shrug off, say, someone burning an American flag). As Mencken wrote, "All of us, to be sure, cherish delusions, but it is at least possible for a rational man to avoid the more gross and obvious ones."

You *can* clarify your thinking. In a world soaked through with abstractions, general semantics will help you clarify your thinking to a degree you would not have been able to do unaided. I see it in my own thinking, using these ideas. As the old saying goes, "if I can do it, you can do it."

Let us push the boundaries even further, and then we'll bring it closer to some common-sense practice.

'Civilization' Itself Is a Made-Up Creation

Stock markets, central banks, corporations, the economy, money itself... are all concepts, symbols, ideas, made up by people. The idea of "career success," of making lots of money, of 'working hard' and the hero worship we show to people who hit societal markers... it's all absurd when you think about what's really going on.

Lots of people chasing little green pieces of paper, or representations thereof... All dressed up in their jackets and ties and dresses and heels, hurrying off to do 'important' things. People sitting in traffic... People getting stressed out... All because symbols and ideas, essentially myths, push them to work and consume, in a never-ending cycle for more, more, more...

Perhaps the most sustained and extreme critiques of civilization and symbols come from author John Zerzan. In his collection of essays titled *Elements of Refusal*, Zerzan attacks how we let words and symbols rule over us.

He writes, "grammar is the invisible 'thought control' of our invisible prison." Language conceals, justifies, lies... "Language stands behind all of the massive legitimation necessary to hold civilization together," he writes. Our own mental contraptions turn us away from the natural world, from the world "out there" and instead turn our attention on the world in our heads. "Life in civilization is lived almost wholly in a medium of symbols."

These are not new ideas. The historian Oswald Spengler (1880-1936) recognized the power of language when he wrote; "to name anything by a name is to win power over it." And we can go back all the way to Plato's Cave, where people watch shadows on the wall and name them and make these shadows their reality.

But I like how Zerzan roots his work in anthropology and history. You don't have to agree with everything he writes to find merit in his research. He shows how the idea we have of a 'working economy' – even the idea of work itself – did not spring naturally. The idea of a 'capitalistic economy' – the idea of a job – is an idea that had to be fought for and won.

Even in mainstream books, such as Juliet Schor's *The Overworked American*, you can see it took a lot of effort over centuries to get people used to the idea of showing up at a certain time and place to "work." It took centuries to get people to accept the idea of regular hours, and so much time off for lunch or for leisure. Monday morning blues? Forget it, they had Saint Monday – a common day off.

For modern life to emerge, the powers that be had to tame and defang the less regimented culture that preceded it.

It was not so long ago that craftsman worked when they needed to work. Leisure time was more plentiful. Medieval calendars were filled with holidays and festivals. Time itself was approximate, governed by the sun and the change in seasons, not the clock. There was no 'work day,' no hours or minutes.

Public clocks began to make their appearance in the 1300s. And people did not greet their arrival with enthusiasm. Historian Merritt Roe Smith writes, "the idea of a clocked day seemed not only repugnant but an outrageous insult to their self-respect and freedom."

So, it was no surprise when early peasants revolted they would destroy the town clock. Again, it took centuries to get people to buckle under to the idea of a 'boss.' In the early days of factory work, absenteeism was a real problem. People frequently didn't show up for work on time. By the 1830s, Zerzan writes, factory life had won its survival. But history could have gone differently.

(If you're ever feeling a little smug about our great technological civilization, spend a little time with Zerzan. *The Elements of Refusal* has his best work. But see also *Against Civilization,* which he edited. It collects essays from a wide range of contributors).

Thus, our most basic ideas about the way we think about 'civilization' are a bunch of abstractions, or mental concepts. They're fictions, in the same way novels are. They're stories we tell ourselves. They are a kind of self-made illusion. The German philosopher Max Stirner (1806-1856) charmingly referred to our self-made illusions as "spooks." (Actually, Stirner wrote in German and the term spooks we owe to his translator, Steven Byington.)

Stirner is worth a mention here. He seemed fascinated by reification, or the process of how we take beliefs, taboos, etc. and let them hold sway over our thinking as if they were actual physical chains or restraints. He spends many pages exploring reification. "Man, your head is haunted," he wrote.

To Stirner, anything you held sacred was a fetter, a "fixed idea." You could only slip this fetter when you have "no misgiving about bringing [your idea] in danger of death at every moment." Stirner liked the taste of having his own ideas bloodied and knocked down:

> I shall look forward smilingly to the outcome of the battle, smilingly lay the shield on the corpses of my thoughts and my faith, smilingly triumph when I am beaten. That is the very humor of the thing.

In markets, you see many people with 'fixed ideas.' They are the ones who never change their mind. They are the ones who you can nearly always predict what they're going to say before they even say it.

I try to have no attachment to ideas and thus I should have no problem changing my mind. To get to this state, though, it helps to see abstractions as abstractions, as ideas people create, as maps. And maps leave things out, etc., as we've discussed in these pages.

We make maps of everything. Even the idea of nations is an abstraction. Alan Watts asks us to consider the Earth as viewed from space. It's a palette of color, mostly blue and green, but also white, yellow, brown... Now consider a political map, "angrily scratched across with straight lines... covered with patches of contrasting colors to identify domains of differing bands of gangsters."

Of course, this doesn't mean you should go around ignoring borders and getting into trouble. But it does help foster a more detached attitude about it all. People who wave flags around yelling suddenly appear ridiculous. The nationalistic appeals of politicians seem absurd. (It reminds me of the Seinfeld bit, where he says loyalty to any one team is hard to justify. You are actually rooting for laundry. "That guy is no good; he's wearing a different shirt! Boo!")

It doesn't mean you can't join in the fun, you just realize it's an abstraction. And knowing this tempers your emotional involvement and therefore helps keep your wits and sanity when other people lose theirs. Those guys who get in fights at international soccer matches? They must rank near the height of human stupidity. Getting all worked up over what...? A bunch of abstractions. They have spooks in their head.

Even in more 'serious' matters of war, I wonder. I have a mild interest in military history and I always marvel at why people did what they did. Standing in the

How Do You Know?

fields at Antietam, where a 19-year-old ancestor fought, I think about how crazy the whole thing seems. Antietam was the site of the bloodiest single-day battle of the Civil War – not just of the Civil War, but of American history. Thousands of men lined up to kill each other. Why didn't they all just walk off and forget the whole thing? Tell the generals to stuff it and head off to the nearest bar or go home to their families? You had to have your head filled with spooks – abstract notions of patriotism and politics and loyalty and honor, etc. – to be there at all.

We're a strange species. I look out my window and see the squirrels playfully chasing each other in the trees. No group of squirrels would ever band together to put certain other squirrels in gas chambers. It takes a lot of spooks in your head to do that.

I'm not immune to abstractions. I spend a lot of time studying stocks and trying to value businesses – all abstractions to varying degrees. But I enjoy this work – it often doesn't feel like work, more like play. And I go at it in a detached manner, which probably contributes to my 'success' as an investor. It's easier to be cool and rational and patient when you don't take any of it too seriously.

I don't want to belabor this point too much, but you'll receive many benefits when you see through life's charades. If you have no "sacred cows" you inevitably shed a lot of anxiety and hang-ups other people lug around with them. I won't go so far as to say you'll be happier. But I can't see how you won't at least feel calmer, less anxious, less neurotic, and generally enjoy a more balanced, rational, carefree disposition. What I offer here is a pushback on the chronic anxiety of our age.

Everything Is Connected

Let us get back to pushing the boundaries of what we've learned so far. Let's explore the thin-aired space on the frontiers...

Remember the chain index we discussed earlier? The index, you may recall, places a thing as unique, such as investor$_1$, investor$_2$, etc. We can talk about investors as a class, but the index reminds us they are all different individually. The chain index adds an additional qualifier to remind us that the thing (in this case 'investor') is not even the same as itself in different environments and contexts. So, for example, investor$_{1\text{ trading his personal account at home}}$ is not the same as investor$_{1\text{ investing his clients' money at the office}}$.

The chain index says your environment is an essential part of 'who you are' at any moment. You cannot separate yourself from your surroundings. You cannot exist in a vacuum. You require space and time, and air, etc. We're like trees in a field. You can imagine a tree, but you also need the sky, the soil, the rain, the air, etc. In short, you need it all.

You can't escape the connectedness of everything. Alan Watts once used the metaphor of a saw. We think the tips of the teeth do the cutting. But you need the valleys in between or there are no teeth. We need the tips of the teeth *and* the valleys in between.

The sages of old knew this.

Vedantic philosophy teaches we are all manifestations of the same consciousness, or leaves off the same tree. Or put another way, there is a substratum that connects us all together. As the wise man Annamalai Swami said: "If you see a carved wooden elephant, for example, you see the form of the carving, your mind registers 'elephant' and you forget that it is wood... It is the same when you see jewelry made out of gold," he said. "You see a shape, call it a ring or a necklace, and while you are studying the form, you temporarily forget the substance it is made of."

And so it is with people – we seem different, but we're all of the same stuff and connected in countless ways. One more analogy may help you get the feel of this idea, again from Alan Watts:

> Think of the nerves in your body – there are billions and billions of them. Now imagine that at the end of each nerve is a little eye that gets an impression of the world and sends the information back to a central brain. This is more like the Hindu idea.

I find this idea fascinating. It is a hard idea to explain or to logically get a firm hold of, which is why I prefer to speak of it in analogies. What I am talking about is more a feeling, or intuition, about how everything connects – not just people, but everything – even if we don't see it at the moment. I suspect those wise old Indian philosophers were onto something.

The idea of connectedness advocates for a holistic approach, which is not easy to adopt.

"Holistic thinking is difficult," author Robert S. de Ropp writes. "It involves thinking about whole systems and seeing the connections between holons at different levels. [A holon is something that is simultaneously a whole and a part. Arthur Koestler coined the term in his book *The Ghost in the Machine*, per Wikipedia]. There are many of these levels. Subatom, atom, molecule, organelle, organism, ecosystem, biosphere, planet, sun, galaxy, all these are holons. All interact. All must be taken into account."

Which is impossible, really. We can't take everything into account. But in finance, we love to pull things apart and isolate 'causes.' Low interest rates cause this. High economic growth causes that. We're constantly trying to model the world as if one lever pulled here causes something else to happen over there. The world does not seem to work that way.

If everything is connected, then the idea of cause and effect becomes very murky indeed, if it even makes any sense at all. Things just happen and there may be no real reason that we can discern.

The mystic G.I. Gurdjieff put this in a memorable way:

> Everything happens. All that befalls a man, all that is done by him, all that comes from him—all this happens. And it happens in exactly the same way as rain falls as a result of a change in the temperature in the higher regions of the atmosphere or the surrounding clouds, as snow melts under the rays of the sun, as dust rises with the wind.

People often react negatively to these kinds of ideas. If everything happens then no one really 'does' anything. So much for the self-help industry and those fawning articles on CEOs and entrepreneurs! So much for the "look at me" culture rife on Facebook and Twitter.

You can get into deep philosophical waters here, but let us bring this back to investing.

If everything is connected, then you must naturally distrust all cause-and-effect thinking. Theories of any kind should be held loosely and with skepticism. As Myron Scholes, the Nobel Prize-winning financial theorist, once said: "We make models to abstract reality. But there is a meta-model beyond the model that assures us that the model will eventually fail. Models fail because they fail to incorporate the inter-relationships that exist in the real world."

How Do You Know?

Do not be deceived by impressive analysis – those 100-page slide decks, those arrays of numbers and charts, the glitter of Wall Street and PhDs and government statistics.

This reminds me how often I will walk out of a meeting with fellow investors and think, "they don't know any more than I do." They may pretend they know a lot, but this is a conceit. They often know more pointless details. I know analysts who could tell you what the CEO eats for breakfast, but still lost money in the stock. I exaggerate, but the point stands.

One of the money managers who made this point well was Martin Sosnoff.

Sosnoff was a money manager for more than 50 years. He grew up in the tenements in the Bronx and served in the Korean War. His books, which are part punchy memoir and part investing guide, are quotable and fun to read. I have well-marked copies of his *Humble on Wall Street* and *Silent Investor, Silent Loser* and his latest, *Master Class for Investors*.

A running theme is the futility of relying too heavily on facts and figures. His first law is "the price of a stock varies inversely with the thickness of the research file." Really good ideas are often strong enough to overpower the finer details.

Sosnoff was an art buff and he drew the line connecting the principles of good investing to Barnett Newman's reductionist paintings. For Sosnoff, investing is also an exercise in minimalist art. Money is not made in the decimal points of spreadsheets. "Conceptual power is everything," as Sosnoff says. I believe you can boil down your success in any investment to just a few key variables. And if you can't do that, you don't understand the idea as well as you think.

Knowledge does not translate into profits; often knowledge seems a curse. You can 'know' too much. Especially, as the old phrase has it, if what you know isn't so. Or what you know just isn't important.

Another way you can see how unimportant most things are: think about how much you forget. Think about the constant chatter that goes on every day in financial markets. About 99% of it you can't remember weeks later, even days later, even hours later... And yet, at the time, whatever it was seemed important. These episodes of forgetting beg the question of how important any of what happened was in the first place. Noodling over it, you come to realize not much is really important at all. Nor, as that holistic approach implies, do you have much control over what happens anyway.

If that's right, then it seems pointless to get upset or stressed or mentally unravel over the issue of the moment. (I tell myself this when I miss a short putt...)

The Courage to Stand Alone

Q: "If you were to sum up your teaching in one phrase, what would it be?"

A: "The phrase would be, 'I cannot help you.'"

~ U.G. Krishnamurti

U.G. Krishnamurti (1918-2007) was a most unusual thinker. He rejected much of what modern life was about. He had no 'job' per se for most of his adult life, no particular ambitions or attachments to things.

As a young man he sought spiritual 'enlightenment.' From those adventures he came to think there was no such thing as enlightenment and developed a sharp skepticism about almost everything. He was a great talker and soon word got around. People would come from all over the world to see him and ask him questions about life, death, meaning, and all sorts of things.

He never charged anybody any money to see him. It wasn't a business. He seemed to have few possessions and he traveled frequently, staying with friends and others who wished to host him.

He wrote no books, but several of his talks or conversations have been transcribed and published by fans. I've enjoyed these books as well as many videos of these conversations posted on YouTube. U.G., as people call him, is funny, witty, and sometimes absurd and silly, but never boring.

Many of our themes run through his talks – for example, the mistrust of cause-and-effect type thinking.

U.G. likes to use the word "acausal." There are so many things happening in nature, for example, which cannot be attributed to any particular cause. Think of lightning. Why does lightning strike where it does when it does? We don't really know. Yes, we have a scientific explanation – anybody can Google it. But just ask another "why" or two, and we're stumped.

U.G. also seemed to relish piercing through words and abstractions. He saw that much of what we know and believe has been put there by other people, by the cultures we're raised in. He saw how we could create our own problems by inventing ideals and trying to be something other than what we are.

I find people have very different reactions to U.G. Some people get upset and even angry at him, or mock him. And I suppose I understand why: they have deep emotional attachments to ideas and here is a guy telling them those ideas are mostly nonsense.

I am, however, mostly amused by U.G. If I could impart one character trait on you, my reader, it would be a healthy sense of humor. Laugh more. Life may not be a joke, but it is often funny. If you keep in mind the abstractions, most of the serious business of the world seems pretentious, trivial, silly, and ridiculous. You can't help but laugh at it.

In my office, I have several laughing Buddhas. I picked up the first one when I was in China in 2005. I remember seeing it on the dashboard of a taxicab. I asked the driver about it. The driver told me that the laughing Buddha reminded him that nothing really mattered and to laugh at the world's troubles.

I was so smitten with the message I bought a little Buddha carving at my next stop. I've since collected a bunch of them. I have one in my car, one on my nightstand and a handful sprinkled in my office. Perhaps a reminder of your own choosing will help you keep perspective.

Now, before I end this book, I must at last ask one big question: What does it matter if you 'succeed' or not as an investor?

I ask you to give it some thought.

Many foster an illusion in thinking things will be better if they had more money. Things will be different, that much we know. (It's one of our four basic propositions.) But human beings seem hardwired not to be content. Whatever you achieve, you will always want more. Societal and biological pressures will still tickle your wants and needs, play on your anxieties and fears, and spark your vanity to keep you playing the game as before.

It may seem difficult to resist all these siren songs. It requires courage. One collection of U.G.'s talks bears the title *The Courage to Stand Alone*. The book ends this way:

> You can have the courage to climb the mountain, swim the lakes and go on a raft to the other side of the Atlantic or Pacific. That any fool can do. But the courage to be on your own, to stand on your own two solid feet, is something which cannot be given by somebody. If you are freed from the burden of the entire past of mankind, then what is there is the courage.

Courage isn't giving in to what others expect or tell you to do and think. Courage is not giving in. I think U.G. is right when he says nobody can give you this kind of courage. But I hope this book gives you the tools whereby you may find that courage.

What I am calling for is a radical rethinking of everything we think we know. What I am calling for is repeated use of the question "How do you know?"

Ask it, and ask it often.

Wendell Johnson, the general semanticist we met earlier, wrote, "The value of a book is not in the book, it is in the subsequent behavior of its readers."

Which means the value of this book is for you to judge. Maybe this book didn't push you all the way into Chapel Perilous. But I'd like to think I nudged you, even if just a bit, in the direction of humility about what you know and that I got you to think about that little question: "How do you know?"

Bibliographic Essay – Recommended Reading

I owe a great debt to a number of books and thinkers. Below, I'd like to recommend some of the ones I found most helpful. If you've not read any of these books, you have quite the intellectual feast ahead of you.

Let's start with general semantics. I would not begin your studies with Korzybski's *Science and Sanity*. It is not an easy read. You may want to start with *Drive Yourself Sane* by Bruce Kodish, which is a simple introduction to general semantics.

In my experience, Kodish is always a reliable source on general semantics. He is also Korzybski's biographer. If you want to read more about Korzybski the man, read Kodish's excellent *Korzybski: A Biography*. This book serves as a good overview of general semantics, too, and its development. Highly recommended.

But I would encourage you to eventually read Korzybski in his own words. You could start with *General Semantics Seminar 1937*. It's an edited transcript of a series of lectures Korzybski gave at Olivet College. Here you can read Korzybski speaking in a more colloquial way about his some of his ideas.

I had a false start when I first tried to read *Science and Sanity*. But my instincts told me the book was special and had treasures worth prying loose. After reading the *Seminar* book, I again tried *S&S* and this time I made it through. You just have to be patient and go at it slow. It will be easier after you've read the *Seminar* book and/or *Drive Yourself Sane*.

Another introductory text I found very useful is *A General Semantics Glossary: Pula's Guide for the Perplexed* by Robert P. Pula. He explains, in little mini-essays, various terms used in general semantics as well as bigger-picture ideas on topics such as validity and truth, uncertainty, etc. Pula taught general semantics for some 40 years and it shows. He's honed the essentials of the discipline to great clarity. Pula has a sense of humor as well. He also strikes me as wise. All in all, it's a delightful companion for your exploration of general semantics.

There are also a number of writers who attempted to write more accessible, popular treatments of general semantics. I'm partial to Irving Lee's *Language Habits in Human Affairs*. I'd also recommend Lee's "Talking Sense" presentation, which you can find on YouTube. Wendell Johnson's *People in Quandaries* is out of print, but worth tracking down if you want another readable treatment of general semantics.

Harry Weinberg's *Levels of Knowing and Existence* is a more intermediate text, but very good. The back half of the book, in particular, has some thoughtful chapters on religion, the mystic experience, the fear of death, Zen, cybernetics, and more – all examined using general semantics.

Another intermediate-level text, and one of my favorite books on general semantics, is Gad Horowitz's *The Book of Radical General Semantics*. Horowitz (and his contributors) come up with a number of memorable examples and demonstrations, and push general semantics to explore areas such as modern politics, myth, art, religion, and other "tough" areas. His section on the meaning of anti-Semitism is the sanest thing I've ever read on the topic. There are fascinating discussions on the idea of self, self-esteem, and the notion of free will. Highly recommended after you've digested a couple of the introductory texts.

So, that's the core of what I'd recommend in general semantics. Once you've read the above, you will find your way to other books and articles of interest.

Now, I want to mention two other thinkers (both influenced by Korzybski) who have had a big impact on my thinking and whose influence runs throughout this book.

I'll start with Robert Anton Wilson, or RAW to his fans. He claims that Korzybski influenced him more than any other writer. You can see that influence in his writings. And it was my reading of RAW that first piqued my interest in Korzybski and general semantics. To me, RAW's philosophy represents a playful agnosticism; a willingness to doubt and play with ideas, without a commitment to believe or not believe, no matter how strange at first. His books are also "doorway" books, in that they will surely introduce you to people and ideas you may never have encountered otherwise. I'm fairly certain I never would have picked up a book about (or by), say, Aleister Crowley, if I hadn't read RAW first.

I recommend RAW's trio *Cosmic Trigger*, *Quantum Psychology*, and *Prometheus Rising*. These books contain some of his best work, in my view. Even if you never pick up a book of his, I'd urge to at least read his preface to *Cosmic Trigger*, which you can find for free online. If there is a more succinct and eloquent statement of the skeptical philosophy in this book, I don't know about it. Reading RAW is a mindbender, and not for everyone, but if you enjoy having your view of reality stretched and challenged, RAW is great fun.

Second, there is Alan Watts, who is perhaps most famous for popularizing Eastern religions and attitudes in the West. But to think of him in just those terms, as I used to do before I became an avid reader and fan, does not do his work justice in the least. Watts was a poetic writer, carving out beautiful sentences laced with unforgettable metaphors and similes. And his books are full of penetrating wisdom about the big questions, about how we might think about our place in the universe.

You can pick up any of his books and find much to chew on and ponder. You'll also see the influence of Korzybski. RAW once interviewed Watts for *The Realist* – RAW and Watts were friends – and had an exchange about general semantics:

> *The Realist*: "How would you evaluate the relationship between Zen and General Semantics?"
>
> Alan Watts: "Well, there's a very close tie in principle between Zen and General Semantics, but there is a great difference in practice. Most semantics people I know talk too much and get increasingly involved in increasingly fine distinctions, as if language could be made n-dimensional. But I do think many of the writers—Korzybski, Bois, Hayakawa—have said things to wake people up. I'm all for General Semantics as long as they call a halt to the discussion at about eleven o'clock."

You can see here Watts' sense of humor and light touch – never seeming to take anything too seriously. Admirable traits. His books are often deceptively short. You'll find yourself stopping over certain passages to think. A slender 120-page book that you expected to zip through in a day or two instead lingers. I haven't read a Watts book yet that I didn't enjoy and want to re-read. But some good places to start include *The Book, The Wisdom of Insecurity, Out of Your Mind*, and *Psychotherapy East and West.*

There are too many good passages to quote from and my Watts books have many starred passages, but I tried to choose something that might summarize Watts' general attitude. Here it is, from *Out of Your Mind*: "Our very existence is rhythm – waking, sleeping, eating, moving. And what's it all about? Does it really mean anything? Does it go anywhere? Fundamentally, the world is play."

The world is play. Have fun and happy reading!

How Do You Know?

Selected Bibliography

Bamberger, W.C. *Adelbert Ames, Jr.: A Life of Vision and Becomingness.* Whitmore Lake, MI: Bamberger Books, 2006.

Bateson, Gregory. *Mind and Nature: A Necessary Unity.* Cresskill, NJ: Hampton Press, 2002.

Berman, Sanford I., and Oliver Leslie Reiser. *Logic and General Semantics: Writings of Oliver L. Reiser and Others.* San Francisco, CA: International Society for General Semantics, 1989.

Bois, Joseph Samuel, and Gary David. *The Art of Awareness: A Handbook on Epistemics and General Semantics.* Fourth ed. Santa Monica, CA: Continuum Press & Productions, 1996.

Bourland, D. David, and Paul Dennithorne Johnston. *To Be or Not: An E-Prime Anthology.* San Francisco, CA: International Society for General Semantics, 1991.

Chisholm, Francis Perry. *Introductory lectures on general semantics: a transcription of a course given at the Institute of General Semantics.* Englewood, NJ: Institute of General Semantics, 1991.

Chrystal, Ellen J. *The Courage to Stand Alone: Conversations with U.G. Krishnamurti.* New Delhi: New Age, 2002.

Evans, Harold. *Do I Make Myself Clear? Why Writing Well Matters.* New York, NY: Little, Brown And Company, 2017.

Hayakawa, S.I., and Alan Hayakawa. *Language in Thought and Action.* Fifth ed. USA: Harvest Original, 1991.

Heuer, Richards J. *Psychology of Intelligence Analysis.* USA: Center for the Study of Intelligence, 1999.

Horowitz, Gad, and Shannon Bell. *The Book of Radical General Semantics.* New Delhi: Pencraft International, 2016.

Johnson, Kenneth G. *General Semantics: An Outline Survey.* Fort Worth, TX: Institute of General Semantics, 2004.

Johnson, Wendell. *People in Quandaries: The Semantics of Personal Adjustment.* San Francisco, CA: International Society for General Semantics, 1946.

Keyes, Ken. *How to Develop Your Thinking Ability*. New York, NY: McGraw-Hill, 1979.

Kodish, Susan Presby, Bruce I. Kodish, and Albert Ellis. *Drive Yourself Sane: Using the Uncommon Sense of General Semantics*. Pasadena: Extensional Publishing, 2011.

Kodish, Bruce I. *Dare to Inquire: Sanity and Survival for the 21st Century and Beyond*. Pasadena, CA: Extensional Publishing, 2003.

Kodish, Bruce I. *Korzybski: A Biography*. Pasadena, CA: Extensional Publishing, 2011.

Korzybski, Alfred. *Manhood of Humanity: The Science and Art of Human Engineering*. Second ed. New York, NY: Dutton, 1921.

Korzybski, Alfred. *General semantics seminar 1937: Transcription of notes from lectures in general semantics given at Olivet College*. Third ed. Brooklyn, NY: Institute of General Semantics, 2002.

Korzybski, Alfred. *Collected Writings, 1920-1950*, edited by M. Kendig. Englewood, NJ: Institute of General Semantics, 1990.

Korzybski, Alfred. *Science and Sanity: An Introduction to Non-Aristotelian Systems and General Semantics*. Fifth ed. Fort Worth, TX: Institute of General Semantics, 2005.

Krishnamurti, U.G., Antony Paul Frank Noronha, J.S.R.L Narayana Moorty, and Sunita Pant. Bansal. *Thought is Your Enemy: Conversations with U.G. Krishnamurti*. New Delhi: Winsome Books India, 2009.

Krishnamurti, U.G., and Rodney Arms. *The Mystique of Enlightenment: The Radical Ideas of U.G. Krishnamurti*. Boulder, CO: Sentient Publications, 2002.

Krishnamurti, Jiddu, and D. Rajagopal. *Think on These Things*. New York, NY: Harper & Row, 1964.

Lee, Irving J. *Language Habits in Human Affairs*. New York, NY: Harper, 1941.

Lev, Baruch, and Feng Gu. *The End of Accounting and the Path Forward for Investors and Managers*. Hoboken, NJ: Wiley, 2016.

MacNeal, Edward. *Mathsemantics: Making Numbers Talk Sense*. New York, NY: Penguin Books, 1995.

Pula, Robert P. *A General-Semantics Glossary: Pula's Guide for the Perplexed*. Concord, CA: International Society for General Semantics, 2000.

Rosenzweig, Phil. *The Halo Effect …and the Eight Other Business Delusions That Deceive Managers*. New York, NY: Free Press, 2014.

Sawin, Gregory. *Thinking & Living Skills: General Semantics for Critical Thinking*. Concord, CA: International Society for General Semantics, 1995.

Stirner, Max. *The Ego and His Own*. Brooklyn, NY: Verso, 2014.

Swami, Annamalai, and David Godman. *Final Talks*. Boulder, CO: Avadhuta Foundation, 2015.

Sword, Helen. *The Writer's Diet: A Guide to Fit Prose*. Chicago, IL: The University of Chicago Press, 2016.

Watts, Alan. *In My Own Way: An Autobiography*. Novato, CA: New World Library, 2007.

Watts, Alan. *The Book: On the Taboo Against Knowing Who You Are*. New York, NY: Vintage, 1989.

Watts, Alan. *Psychotherapy East & West*. Novato, CA: New World Library, 2017.

Watts, Alan. *Cloud-Hidden, Whereabouts Unknown: A Mountain Journal*. New York, NY: Vintage, 1974.

Watts, Alan. *Out of Your Mind: Tricksters, Interdependence, and the Cosmic Game of Hide-and-Seek*. Boulder, CO: Sounds True, 2017.

Weinberg, Harry L. *Levels of Knowing and Existence: Studies in General Semantics*. Englewood, NJ: Institute of General Semantics, 1987.

Whorf, Benjamin Lee. *Language, Thought, and Reality: Selected Writings of Benjamin Lee Whorf*, edited by John B. Carroll, Penny Lee, and Stephen C. Levinson. Cambridge, MA: MIT Press, 2012.

Wilson, Robert Anton. *Cosmic Trigger I*. Grand Junction, CO: Hilaritas Press, 2016.

Wilson, Robert Anton. *Quantum Psychology*. Grand Junction, CO: Hilaritas Press, 2016.

Wilson, Robert Anton. *Prometheus Rising*. Grand Junction, CO: Hilaritas Press, 2016.

Zerzan, John. *Elements of Refusal*. Columbia, MO: CAL Press, 2006.

Index

A

abracadabra, 7, 14, 17

Abramović, Marina, 119, 123

absolutist (absolutistic)

 approach to what we believe, 36

 "Is that really so?," 170

 language fosters discontent, 182

 terms, avoid, 170

abstractions. *See also* delayed reactions; map(s); words and symbols

 across space-time, 36

 awareness of, 191–92, 197

 category building, 15

 civilization as, 201

 concrete nouns *vs.,* 102

 distrust, 61

 evaluate higher-order, 152

 fuzzy thinking, 102, 104

 "growth stocks," 20

 heavy, 39

 idea of nations, 202

 ideas, concepts, theories, definitions, 25

 identify and pierce, 8

 intrinsic value of a business, 75

 limitations of our, 23, 29

 map of the U.S., 24

 "stocks are going to go up/down," 13

 thinking mindfully of, 7

 "Value Investing Hits Back," 9–10

 "value stocks," 20

 Wall Street, 7, 9

Ackman, Bill, 92, 149

Adams, Douglas, 61

Adams, Scott, 87

additive principles, 18

advertisements, 192–93

Against Civilization (Zerzan), 201

All PowerShares, 57

American flag, 199, 202

American Revolution, 16

Ames Jr., Adelbert, 62–64, 73

Ames Room, 62–63

anthropomorphists, 30

Antietam, Battle of, 203

anti-Semitism, 212

Apple (AAPL), 12

Arcos Dorados, 143

Aristotelian

 assumptions, 27

 logic, 25–26

 non-Aristotelian *vs.,* 25–29

 orientation, 25, 27

 systems, 26, 38

assumptions

 Aristotelian, 27

 economy's growth rate, 44

 embedded, 116–17

 faulty/false, 20, 81, 84

 Newton *vs.* quantum physics, 28

 silent, 8

Atatürk, Mustafa Kemal, 77

Attorneys.com, 57

average

 better-than-average results, 4

 concept of, 42

 Dow Jones Industrial Average, 85

 investors underperformed market, 183

 markets, 41

 price-earnings ratios, 41–42, 106

 in real life, 42

 return of Templeton Growth Fund, 183

 S&P 500 trades, 134

 Standard & Poor companies, 132–33

B

Bakalar, Nicholas, 56
Bamberger, W.C., 62
Bateson, Gregory, 198–99
Beck, Kristine, 51
BeerAdvocate website, 121
behavioral finance, 72
Behavioural Investing: A Practitioner's Guide to Applying Behavioural Finance (Montier), 72
Berkshire Hathaway, 19, 41, 105, 134–35
Berman, Sanford, 16
biological realities, 132
Blackstone, 135–36
Boeing *vs.* Lockheed Martin, 159–60
Bonner, Bill, 1–4, 82
The Book of Radical General Semantics (Horowitz), 25, 47–48, 185, 212
The Book: On the Taboo Against Knowing Who You Are (Watts), 43, 209
books, recommended, 28, 211–13
Bourland, D. David, 166–68
Braniff International Airways, 77
Brawley, Louis, 53
Bregman, Steven, 11, 53
Bridgman, P.W., 98
Brown, Ken *(The Wall Street Journal)*, 57
Buddhas, laughing, 208
Buffett, Warren, 19, 42, 105, 134, 183
Built to Last: Successful Habits of Visionary Companies (Collins and Porras), 49–50
Bukowski, Charles, 39
Bush, George W., 174
business
  abstract language, 102–3
  Berkshire Hathaway, 19, 41, 105, 134–35

Big Mac, 173
Coca-Cola, 149, 173
delusions, 48–51
differences across time and place, 144
diverse portfolio of, 106
forget the bottom line, 160
gold mining shares, 85
good, different ideas about, 98
intrinsic value of, 75
performance, 50
buybacks, 41, 135

C

calendars, medieval, 201
CAPE ratio, 41–42
capitalistic economy, 200
Carmichael, R.D., 61
Carroll, John B., 114
Carroll, Lewis, 82
Cassel, Ian, 77
cause and effect
  business delusions, 48–52
  cat and tail analogy, 43, 52
  causation, multi-faceted *vs.* single antecedent, 66
  CEO performance, 66
  chance and happenstance, 43
  chosen set of data points, 43
  complexities of markets and life, 39
  complexity of our world, 8
  connecting the dots, 47–48
  data mining, futility of, 41–42
  distrust, learn to, 39, 51
  everything is connected *vs.*, 205
  in financial markets, 42
  find whatever you want in the data, 42
  "if X then Y" statement, 44, 52

Z

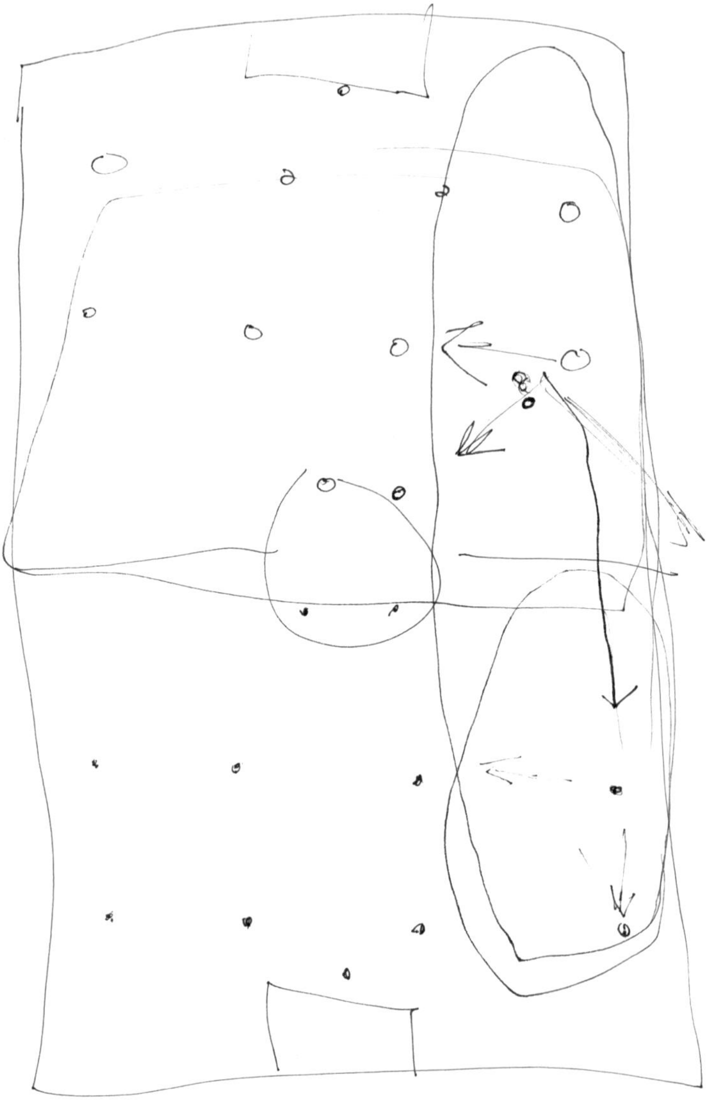

Made in the USA
Monee, IL
03 December 2020